SALT *& Honey*

Jewish Teens

on Feminism,

Creativity,

& Tradition

Edited by Elizabeth Mandel,
Emanuelle Sippy, Maya Savin
Miller, and Michele Lent Hirsch
with the jGirls Magazine Collective

Foreword by Molly Tolsky of
Hey Alma

Reader's Guide by
Michelle Shapiro Abraham

Editorial Consultants

Michelle Shapiro Abraham, Union for Reform Judaism; Tova Harris,
Be'chol Lashon; Andrea Jacobs, Rally Point; Tani Prell, 18Doors; Dr. Betsy Stone,
Hebrew Union College

The jGirls Magazine Collective

Editors: Elizabeth Mandel, Emanuelle Sippy, Maya Savin Miller, Michele Lent Hirsch

Additional Writing and Editing: Annie Poole, Aydia Caplan, Audrey Honig, Katina
    Paron

Content Curation: Aydia Caplan, Cecelia Ross, Elena Eisenstadt, Lily Pazner,
    Reggie Hopkins

Administrative and Creative Support: Annie Poole, Carolyn Kettig, Sara Bogomolny

Additional Support: Alex Berman, Aidyn Levin, Dalia Heller, Joelle Reiter,
    Naomi Kitchen, Sonja Lippmann, Zoe Lanter, and the 2019-2020 & 2020-2021
    jGirls Magazine Teen Staff & Alums

Published by Behrman House, Inc.
Millburn, NJ 07041
www.behrmanhouse.com

ISBN 978-1-68115-077-2

Thank you to the editors of the journals where these pieces first appeared in different form:
"Growing Up Girl" in 805 Literary Magazine, "How to Label Yourself" in Hypernova Lit,
"Here Lie Our Bones" in Sierra Nevada Review and Gallaudet Press, "The Art of Jewish
Food" in JCC Chicago Instagram: Teen Art Competition Series, "Asian Jew or Jewish
Asian?" in The Shofar, Eva in Teen Ink Magazine, "A Message from a Jew with a Touch of
Color" in the Pittsburgh Jewish Chronicle, Mending the Broken (select photos) in the Stuyvesant
Spectator, and "Two Lefts and Then a Right On Orange Grove Boulevard" in Cargoes.

The publisher gratefully acknowledges Shutterstock for the following images:
Cover and Interior p. 1, 3, 27, 57, 85, 111, 133: EngravingFactory; logaryphmic

YOUNG ADULT NONFICTION / Social Topics / Emotions & Feelings

Library of Congress Cataloging-in-Publication Data
Names: Mandel, Elizabeth, 1969- editor.
Title: Salt & honey : Jewish teens on feminism, creativity, & tradition
    / edited by Elizabeth Mandel with jGirls Magazine.
Description: Millburn, NJ : Behrman House, Inc., [2022] | Summary: "This
    collection of poetry, fiction, nonfiction, and art explores what it
    means to be a young Jewish woman today"-- Provided by publisher.
Identifiers: LCCN 2021035886 | ISBN 9781681150772 (paperback)
Subjects: LCSH: Jewish women--Literary collections. | Jewish
    teenagers--Conduct of life. | American literature--Jewish authors. |
    American literature--Women authors.
Classification: LCC PS508.J4 S35 2022 | DDC 810.8/09287089924--dc23
LC record available at https://lccn.loc.gov/2021035886

Design: Zatar Creative
Project Editor: Alef Davis
Printed in the United States of America

Table of Contents

PUBLISHER'S NOTE

We are proud to present these snapshots of the lived experiences of Jewish teens. You will see them living their lives, getting knocked down, rising up, and speaking out (sometimes in poetry). They are declaring in their own voices who they are and who they wish to become.

Some of these writers speak of intense and difficult experiences. Some use raw language, including language that can feel disturbing and even hateful. But words have power. By reporting on the devastating effect some words can have, these writers ultimately reclaim that power. And by choosing their words carefully, using their full and natural voices, they speak with authenticity and strength.

There's much to think about, and to feel, in this book. We hope you'll use the reader's guide at the end to help you consider the issues raised, and to prompt conversations about questions that engage, enlighten, or disturb you, because it's through dialogue that we come to know each other and ourselves.

We hope you find inspiration in the stories of these emerging authors.

David E. Behrman
president, Behrman House

FOREWORD

Long before I knew where exactly my life would take me, I knew what I wanted to be: a writer. A devastatingly shy kid whose eyes would water when a teacher called my name, I found an unexpected power in the written word. There, on the blank page, I could articulate the thoughts I was too terrified to say out loud. There, I was able to write my way to a better understanding of myself.

Still, I felt alone. Filling up pages and pages in my journal could help me work through some internal struggles, but it wasn't until I shared my writing with the world—or, more accurately, a handful of friends and family—that I understood that one of the deeper powers of words was their ability to connect us with one another.

That's why I'm so thrilled that we've been gifted with the collection of writings and art that you're about to experience.

Salt & Honey, a collection of writings and art from jGirls Magazine, empowers Jewish girls, young women, and nonbinary teens by allowing them to put their truth down on paper (or on canvas). The themes explored in this anthology—from childhood to spirituality to sexuality to the world around us—are inherently universal, but it's the specificity found within each story, poem, essay, and work of art that reminds us that being a young Jew today is not a single shared experience. And isn't that a beautiful thing?

That very notion is why I started Hey Alma, a feminist Jewish publication that gives people a platform to share their unique voices and stories with an online community. And it's what makes *Salt & Honey* such a crucial addition to the canon of modern Jewish works.

Within these pages is a representation of the Jewish community at its best: a diversity of voices and experiences; a rigorous commitment to challenging the status quo; creativity; curiosity; humor and heart-break; suffering and joy. That such an invigorating and affirming work was produced by the teens of jGirls Magazine is proof that they've learned a very important lesson early in life: nobody can tell your story but you.

When I read this book, it's impossible not to feel a burst of hope and excitement for the future—of the Jewish community and of our society at large. I'm so grateful for every one of these gifted young writers and artists for not only searching within and filling up that blank page, but for taking the (often terrifying) next step of sharing their stories with us. We are all the better for it.

Molly Tolsky
founding editor, Hey Alma

PREFACE

We are writers, editors, musicians, photographers, and artists. We are multi-ethnic, multiracial, and multifaceted. We prepare the Melida ceremony and dance the hora, bake *dabo* for Sigd, and gather for Mimouna. We brush every crumb from our homes on Passover, and we celebrate Christmas alongside Hanukkah. We live in big urban centers and small rural towns. We enjoy sports, debate, science, camping, and getting out the vote. We have a range of abilities. We love whom we love.

We are fashioned from our words and our brushstrokes; we exist on the page and the canvas and in song. We learn that in Jewish tradition, there are no accidents in language—that every word, every space, every punctuation mark has meaning. The same is true as we construct our identities. We are the stories we tell.

Salt & Honey elevates our stories. We are self-identifying Jewish girls, young women, and nonbinary teens. Because we are so often misunderstood, airbrushed, or flat-out ignored, to tell our own stories is both a revolt and a victory. It is how we challenge and remake who has the right to break the silence and, in doing so, how we create a space that is entirely our own.

Here, we embrace the salt and the honey, the sting and the sweetness, of our lives. We delve into sensitive subjects like mental health and sexuality, giving voice to the realities of our lives without stigmatizing anyone's experience. We showcase the joy that we find in our identities, creativity, activism, and growth. We embrace that we are at once unique individuals and essential pieces of a closely connected community.

We explore this interplay between the individual and the collective and how it lays the foundation for who we are. We start with the past, reflecting on our thousands of years of history and our own childhoods. We move into the present, exploring who we are now. Finally, we look toward the future, examining who we want to become and the world we hope to create.

The works in this book are collected from jGirls Magazine, an online publication and community. Our contributors, all of whom are between the ages of thirteen and nineteen, submit visual art, poetry, essays, music, stories, and short films. Our staff editors and photographers—all in high school—decide collaboratively, in a teens-only space, the content and aesthetic of our magazine. And our readers find resonant stories and new and surprising ways of considering the world. Together, we celebrate the sprawling, messy, complicated, glorious nature of being a young Jewish person today.

In these pages, we hope to make the familiar strange and the strange familiar. We hope you find both a reflection of yourself and a path to new ways of thinking, feeling, and experiencing.

B'ruchot haba'ot! Welcome!

Elizabeth Mandel, Emanuelle Sippy, Maya Savin Miller,
Michele Lent Hirsch, and the jGirls Magazine Collective

Since the liturgy was written:
We learn the words I don't want to claim
The words I love like
salt and honey

FROM "DESIRED BURDEN," BY EMANUELLE SIPPY

1

CHAPTER ONE

We Always Seem to Return

when we capture memories
their paths are prayers of peace

FROM "DESIRED BURDEN," BY EMANUELLE SIPPY

We are inheritors and authors of memory: it's the most powerful heirloom entrusted to us. We carry the stories of those who came before us. We hear history in our songs, see it in our parents' faces, taste it in our grandparents' cooking. We recite the words of our ancestors and remember our responsibility to the next generation.

Our identities unfolded first on loved ones' laps and later around dinner tables full of passionate debate, boisterous laughter, and quiet sorrow. The things we remember are often commonplace: a hug, a shared piece of fruit, a rainy day. Yet the people with whom we share these memories are extraordinary to us. And so, we honor and uplift the voices of those who came before us, ensuring that they are not lost to history. We weave a thread through their stories, our stories, and the stories still to come.

We begin with **One**, collapsing the past and present, the individual and the collective.

Eve: first woman, first mother, first renegade.

In **Held**, the artist develops an intimacy with lost relatives by rendering them in pencil.

We taste a piece of fruit laden with love in **Can You See God in a Grapefruit?**

In **Unmoored from a Mother**, a child contemplates loss while wandering unfamiliar streets.

In **Seeing Beyond**, the writer remembers her complicated relationship with a beloved sister.

We feel the thrill of discovering new family members in **The Half-Mishpocha: Seeking Donor Sibs**.

Family can bring long-lastig pain, as in **Dad**.

Melting into Shards layers meaning and memory.

In **Shattered Glass**, the writer sees herself reflected through her grand-father's eyes and the lens of history.

desired burden spans generations of mothers, daughters, and tradition.

Barbara is a portrait of chosen family.

In **Lemon Steam**, baking a grandmother's recipe evokes her memory in magical, whimsical ways.

One

MAYA RABINOWITZ

You are one in a hundred
And one in a million

A family of land wanderers
With tendriled fingers
Reaching every crack and crevice
Every corner of the planet

You and I
We're not much as fighters
But we know how to pack our bags at night
Or noon
Or how to just leave
With nothing

We starve for a day
And feast for seven

We won't be found
In grit
In spotlight

We live in our heads
Slid between bars of music
In the white space around

And between
And inside
The letters of a story

Through lost grandparents
And lost countries
We always seem
To return

But even today
If the world were a village
Of one hundred—
Of us,

There would be just one.

Eve

TESANEYAH DAN

Held

ALEXA DRUYANOFF

Can You See God in a Grapefruit?

ALIZA ABUSCH-MAGDER

Thousands of juice packets. Sweet, tangy, sour. Packed so closely together in communities commonly called "pieces," and when you hand me a piece of your grapefruit, you hand me a little collection of individuals held together by a thin, opaque, fibrous skin.

When I passed the grapefruit tree on the way to the bank, I effortlessly plucked the ripe, perfumed, leathered teardrop slowly falling from its tired branch.

I casually held a world in my hand, a real-life *Horton Hears a Who!* Don't you see God in Doctor Seuss? Wasn't it divine?

My mama reading me silly rhyming stories, drawing me a bath, handing me a perfectly packed piece of her grapefruit and handing me the peel, all in one, an innocuous fiery pigmented snake with a raw, pale underbelly.

She gave me God from the tips of her fingers directly into my mouth, from the harp of her lips directly into my heart.

When she comes to visit, I will slice open a grapefruit, separate the film from the meat, sprinkle it with sugar.

We will sit together, eating the God we both believe in.

Unmoored from a Mother

AYDIA CAPLAN

Through the glass of a stranger's window,
You look out on a reprising world.
The city rains back onto itself.
A forgotten melody from your infancy
Trails from the curtain.
It no longer lives between your mother's lips
But you meet its timbre again
In the feathery sound of rain.

You walk downstairs in sotto voce and open the front door:
The city smells of thirst and untethered sidewalks.
You are lost. You turn at every corner.
You walk along a stranger's welling streets
As your mother walked before you, and you are lost.

The drizzle beads like goosebumps on your skin.
It feels like suffusion, but only trills along the surface.
The rain rains back onto itself again.

You are lost, you are lost.

Through the treble-shivering glass of a stranger's eyes,
You look out on a key-changed world.
You walk, trilling the surface of the city,
As your mother walked before you and was also lost
And you think of all the ways
A person could die.

Seeing Beyond

LEAH BOGATIE

I have stopped at the edge of a busy street, waiting to cross, when I catch a glimpse of a woman pushing a girl in a wheelchair.

The girl appears to be around ten or eleven. She has short brown hair and brown eyes the color of chocolate. She beams, even though it is an overcast day. Her head is leaning to one side as she sits there, silently.

It is a busy intersection. There are people impatiently waiting for the light to turn green and people rushing to work. However, as the woman walks along with the girl, some begin to stare. Some glance and then quickly look away.

When I see the two of them crossing, my heart catches in my throat. The girl is beautiful, and she takes my breath away. She also reminds me of someone whom I loved dearly. Tears fill my eyes as I drift off into distant memories....

Today is a random day in February. I am twelve, and my older sister is fourteen. She loves to draw, so I have taken out the crayons from the cabinet. There are over thirty colors in the box, ranging from crimson red to deep blue.

I prop the blank paper and the crayon box on the large tray connected to my sister's wheelchair. I ask her, "Devora, what color crayon would you like to start with?"

Devora moves her stiff arm toward the entire box, knocking it off the tray.

I pick up the box, and I try again.

This time, I only put ten crayons on her tray. I repeat my question.

Devora concentrates on the colors in front of her for a few seconds. She then moves her arm toward a group of crayons in the corner of the tray. She is unable to point to the specific color she wants, since her hands remain in fists.

Third time's the charm, I tell myself, as I try a different method. I am beginning to get frustrated, but I try not to let it show. I pick up each crayon individually, stopping to ask her about each.

"Do you like the blue one?" I ask her. She remains quiet and does not smile, which I interpret as a no.

I move on. "How about the pink?" A fraction more excitement begins to show on her face, but I know we are not there yet.

I pick up a third. "What about the purple one?" This time, she cannot contain her excitement. She grins from ear to ear and vocalizes enthusiastically, signaling a yes.

I mentally slap myself. *I should have known purple was the one; it's her favorite color.*

Devora suffered from cerebral palsy, a disorder that affects a person's movement, motor skills, and muscle tone. She was unable to walk or talk, which left her unable to complete normal daily tasks on her own.

Although I adored my sister, it was difficult living with her. She required constant help with eating and bathing, among many other tasks we all take for granted. She would often wake up in the night, crying for hours on end.

My sister was deprived of her freedom, dignity, and independence due to the disorder she was born with. None of it was her fault, yet she was defined by these limitations her entire life. In my experience, most people who met her did not look beyond her cerebral palsy to get to know her better. Perhaps they assumed she did not understand them, so they decided not to try. I would imagine that they did not ascribe much value to her anyway. Moreover, understanding what Devora was trying to communicate required effort, and her capacity to give back to people was limited in return.

I struggled too. As much as I tried to pretend Devora was like any other older sister, I sometimes could not. I was unable to ask her for advice or discuss how her school day went. I could not relate to or empathize with her. I had to learn how to communicate with her in my own way, since she was unable to form proper words.

Despite this, we were still close. We would draw and listen to music together. We would play games and go on walks in the park. I tried hard to be her best friend, because by a young age, I already understood that she might have a hard time being treated equally in society. I always found this unfair, because although she struggled to communicate, she could still understand what was happening around her.

A few months after I forgot to offer her the purple crayon, Devora died. It is unclear why she died so suddenly. I struggled to accept her death for a long time, and, to be completely honest, I am still struggling with it today.

Although Devora had a disability, she was much more than just that. She was kind and creative, and she had a wonderful sense of humor. She was always smiling and cheerful, even when she was sick or recovering from surgery.

Sometimes, what we see on the surface is not the entire picture. Sometimes, it is necessary to dig deeper. What I learned from Devora's brief but meaningful life is that it is important to put ourselves in other people's shoes. If we can only see the world through the lens of our own experiences, we will be stuck in a mindset that will never progress.

I am transported back to reality. I notice the woman and the girl looking at me, and I realize I have been staring. However, I have learned not to turn away from the uncomfortable.

So instead, I stare the girl straight in the eyes.

And I smile.

The Half-Mishpocha
Seeking Donor Sibs

SASHA HOCHMAN

I have always known the truth about being conceived from donor sperm. The idea of knowing my half-brothers and half-sisters had always wandered around in the back of my mind. I daydreamed about walking down a New York City street on a brisk fall day, a scarf wrapped around my neck, and seeing a face similar to mine. I imagined somehow knowing that I shared half the DNA behind that face, and I thought about the happily-ever-after connection between the two of us. But in seventh grade, meeting my siblings never seemed like a plausible reality.

I heard about the Donor Sibling Registry (DSR) from a friend whose moms also used donor sperm to conceive. About a year before, my friend had managed to find and meet her half-siblings on the DSR, an online database for families who used donor sperm. When she told me this at a bar mitzvah party, I was so astonished that I could think of little else, not even my favorite Ke$ha song coming from the dance floor. Meeting my half-siblings didn't have to be a chance encounter, but a decision within my power to make.

The next day, my mom and I sat on the spring-green rug in my room. I gazed at the computer screen before us, set up to register on the site. Anticipation built inside me as waves of unrecognizable emotions wafted to the surface. I continued to stare blankly at the computer screen as my mom typed away. Last and first name. Sperm bank used. Donor number. Type of membership wanted on the Donor Sibling Registry. I reminded myself over and over to take the next breath.

Later that night, less than twenty-four hours after emailing the list of names that came up under donor #448, two alerts popped into my mom's inbox. Two emails that, at the same time, managed to both glare and beam at us: messages from two of my half-siblings.

What was I supposed to say to these people I knew as little about as college calculus, but who shared half of my genetic code? I was in seventh grade at the time, and I remember exchanging questions with my sister

Gracie like, "What do you do in your free time?" and "What's your favorite color?" Pastimes and favorite colors were trivial, but neither of us knew how the script was supposed to look.

As I began to find more of my siblings, I scoured their Instagrams, scrutinizing their pictures. None of them looked like replicas of me or of each other, but here and there I found that we shared the same eyes or the same cheekbones.

Maybe a month after joining the DSR, a new question arose. How many people had successfully conceived with donor #448's sperm? How many half-siblings were there?

In the movie *Delivery Man*, a guy discovers that, after donating sperm in his twenties, he now has five hundred thirty-three offspring. Men with a very high sperm count who donate every week for a year might contribute to thirty pregnancies in that year. It would take decades for them to have five hundred children. However, it's not uncommon for a donor to have upwards of one hundred offspring.

One mom kept a running list of every #448 family that had contacted her, but that's all we had. Parents are not required to report a birth from donor sperm, so there is no accurate count of how many children have been conceived from my donor or anyone else's. Another mom in the #448 group told us she had heard from the sperm bank that there were anywhere from thirty to fifty of us. Even if that wasn't true, I felt bewilderment, maybe wonder, maybe even terror.

One of the #448 moms, we found out, was organizing a meetup. Right around the time we first joined the DSR, she happened to be in the midst of planning it. "Do you want to go?" my mom asked. Of course I wanted to go and meet these people. Of course I wanted to get to know them.

To date, more than 13,102 half-siblings have found each other through the DSR. In an online research study, donor-conceived children were asked about the reasons behind their search for donor siblings. The two main responses were: "curiosity about appearance and personality" and "to know and understand a missing part of me." The study showed that donor offspring made connections with their siblings that were generally positive. Most of the offspring who chose to search for their siblings were open about it with parents, friends, and family. When I searched for my siblings, I did not feel self-conscious or embarrassed. I felt joyous that I had found them, and I wanted to share that joy.

We decided to gather in Boston, with a couple families living there, a couple families driving up, and a couple families driving down. The car ride was long, sweaty, and filled with anticipation.

After parking the car and hauling our belongings into a friend's house, there wasn't much time to get ready. I was stuck. It was the end of summer and eighty degrees outside. Should I wear short-shorts? Should I put makeup on? What were the other girls going to wear? "We need to go in five minutes," one of my moms yelled. I pulled myself together, jammed flip-flops onto my feet, grabbed my phone, and hurtled down the stairs.

Twenty minutes later, after getting three sets of directions to two different addresses and a helpful phone call from one of the #448 parents, we pulled into the gravel driveway, a big wraparound porch staring at us ominously. We were hesitant to open the car doors until a friendly-looking woman appeared from the door and introduced herself as Kathy. "It's so nice to meet you, I'm so glad you finally made it. Come on inside; everyone is already here."

The parents were scattered in small clusters around the house, but all of the half-siblings were seated in the living room. The feeling I had walking into that small, yet immense, gathering of people was like walking into the cafeteria on the first day of school. Meeting them one at a time was hard enough, but since I was the last one there, I was faced with six half-siblings all staring at me. It took a moment to realize that they were smiling and welcoming me in, introducing themselves, and making room on the couch. Their faces were a blur. Manners held me back from staring at them, but I jumped on every chance I had to sneak in glances.

I don't remember what we all talked about—maybe what activities we enjoyed, maybe what we were going to do later. There was a surreal feeling to that living room. It came from the doorway, the cerulean wall paint, the two plush chairs, and the one large couch. It came from the nervous tapping of someone's shoes on the floor and the thick buzz of the ceiling fan. It came from the teeth peeking out from under our smiles and the polite laughter chirping from our throats. Thankfully, it wasn't long before the parents decided it was time to start the evening. After piling into various cars, we made our way over to a picnic below a sky of fireworks.

The families sprawled across numerous blankets, chatting with one another as dinner came to an end. We waited restlessly as shades of deep blue and red swirled into the sky. I don't know which sibling was first to document the moment on Snapchat, but soon we found a bit of the wall dividing us crumble as we exchanged usernames, gathering friends and followers. I sank into the toasty air, comforted by the glowing eyes around me, and watched the fireworks explode into shards of flame.

We ended the night with a trip to a massive ice cream parlor. Again, looking at the menu, I was faced with an array of choices. What was I supposed to order? I didn't want to order a double sundae and look greedy. I didn't want to order vanilla in a dish and look typical. I didn't want to order some made-up flavor decked with candy and nuts and look weird. But eventually, settling down into our various orders, we began to laugh. Most of us were Jewish, only children with lesbian parents. We understood each other's families; we got each other's jokes. None of us had lives at home that matched the ones of our friends with "normal" families. We were all connected by this choice our parents had made. A selection between this vial of sperm or that one.

Our laughter didn't stop until the parents started saying, "It's late, we should call it a night." Even then, we lingered outside the ice cream parlor, bringing our laughter with us, feeling lucky to have each other. I was no longer trying to impress them, no longer worried about what I looked like or what I said. I was allowed to be myself.

I assume that one day I'll meet my donor dad. This, too, seems like a remote scenario playing out in the back corner of my brain. There was once a time when I yearned to have a dad. I felt like there was a hole that needed to be filled. Meeting my siblings filled that hole in a way that I didn't expect. Overnight, I changed from being an only child to being part of a clan. I didn't need a dad or any type of paternal figure. I had siblings.

Dad

DENAE

My mom always told me not to wish people dead, and for the first decade of my life, I never did. But now, I don't know. I think if someone fucks up your life enough, it's kind of inevitable that at some point you'll get so furious that the only thing you *can* do is wish them dead.

I really wish my dad would just bite it already. My money's on death via liver disease or a drunk driving accident...just something involving alcohol. I'm fully aware that my morbid fantasies of my own father's death are exactly that: morbid. Every once in a while, though, during that one day every six months that he decides to text me a paragraph of complete bullshit about how he loves me, I feel awful. My chest feels like it's pinned under a truck, even if only for a moment. And in that moment, I'm guilty. I'm guilty of being a bad daughter, a bad person. I've become increasingly resilient over the years, and I snap out of it rather quickly, but that snap is like a rubber band on my wrist.

The last time I saw him was at a holiday party. I've always dreaded seeing him at family events. For years, I opted out of them: I chose not to take the opportunity to see people who I'd go months—maybe even years—without seeing. All because of him. I thought that if I got over this fear, I'd be a stronger or better person because good, strong people aren't supposed to bail on their families, right?

He tried to hug me. That's what I remember the most. Every harsh "don't touch me" I'd rehearsed in the guest bedroom of my aunt's house suddenly left my mind like sand being yanked out by the tide. "No, I'm good" is all I said. He gave me a seventy-five-dollar gift card to Uniqlo because he didn't know what else to get me. I would've preferred the twenty grand he owed in child support.

He's been texting me more often than he ever has before. Once every two weeks now, but sometimes even more frequently. I wonder if he's ever said something he actually meant. It wouldn't make much of a difference anyway. I keep coming back to him, thinking that maybe this time it's real. I sit on my bed, scrunched over my glaring phone screen, watching my tears fall and distort each character. I do this for about ten minutes until I realize that I need to figure out what my next move is. Usually, it's a word or two. I occasionally manage to shakily type out a decent sentence. It's not the "Fuck you, you're dead to me" I'd like to see in my little blue speech bubble, but it's good enough; at least it's something. It's the best I can do when I'm on the verge of exploding, trying to determine if he's ready to be a good father or if this is yet another one of his abusive, manipulative games.

I don't understand my dad. I've tried interrogating him about why he is the way he is, but all it's resulted in are tears and swearing and an amount of yelling to which no child should ever be subjected. I think if I understood him, I'd sympathize with him, which is the last thing I'd ever want to do. If I sympathized with him, though, maybe I wouldn't want him to die, and then maybe I'd feel like I wasn't evil. I know he doesn't deserve my sympathy. A man who drinks and drives with his children in the car doesn't deserve anything good, to be honest. That's how I see it, at least. For the most part I'm okay with it, but with each ounce of hatred for the man I once loved comes another ounce of guilt and regret. I never wanted to live a life full of regret.

I wonder what my life would be like if I were a more forgiving person. I've come to believe that forgiving someone too many times opens the door to a world of toxicity and abuse. I'd like to think that if I forgave my dad, we'd go right back to where we left off before everything went bad. Bike rides across the Manhattan Bridge and stopping at Bagel World after a day in Fort Greene Park with our dogs. But I'm not that naive. I know who he is, and I know he hasn't changed. It's been a learning process, attempting to cope with the fact that I probably would've been better off with no father. And maybe that's why I wish I didn't have a father now.

Melting into Shards

LIORA MEYER

Shattered Glass

MADISON HAHAMY

Hebrew is a language of swaying trees and rounded edges, of chilly mornings and crackling fireplaces. When my *saba*—my grandfather—speaks it, the syllables roll off his tongue like a knife cutting through softened butter.

Hebrew is a language of glass: sleek, smooth, serene. It is a childhood music box, the soft tinkling notes of the lullaby-esque song continuing on and on and on until it surrenders into the silence. It is my childhood, a blur of sounds both intimately familiar and frustratingly out of reach. It is the language my family speaks when we travel downtown for Shabbat dinner, the language of secrets, reserved for hushed voices after evening conversation has become exhausted.

But when I speak English, my sentences sound like shattered glass, angular fragments that cut and scratch those who step on them. Like the jogger weaving in and out of my peripheral vision, his irregular footsteps paired with labored breathing. Like the siren wailing in agony, falling silent for a brief second and then roaring back to life with more urgency. Like the flashing Ferris wheel that goes round and round, the boisterous music a muffled sound. Like the angry car honking at the unmoving traffic.

Just like shattered glass, my voice sounds rough and disjointed—a gaping chasm between me and my *saba*, me and the language of swaying trees and rounded edges. One that can never be crossed.

A war between the two languages: Hebrew and English. The complete and the broken. The soothing whispers and the harsh wailing. The song of defiance and a song of defeat. Both parts of my being, but only one truly within reach.

I collect my splintered sentences and wait in pensive silence until it is time to hug and kiss my grandparents goodbye. "I love you," my *saba* says. He says it in the language of shattered glass, though his words do not scratch. I look outside toward the winking lights and the unwavering moon. For one moment, the city seems to be holding its breath. "I love you too," I reply. My *saba* smiles. "I love the sound of your voice," he says. "*Yafah.*"

Yafah.

Beautiful.

desired burden

EMANUELLE SIPPY

My mom learned to cook from superstitious women
       I don't know how she learned to pray
And in some sense, that's the essence of prayer

in *chavruta*, shared study

the calm rabbi asked us
to share a memory of togetherness

I said, prayer

Since before I had a name:
Ushering in Shabbat with candles—three gestures
Still and quiet

We should be patient because it is brief

But we are joking because it is sacred
Zach and I elbow each other laughing
       as the match refuses to light
Also a part of the ritual

Since the liturgy was written:
We learn the words I don't want to claim
       The words I love like
salt and honey

Since I heard the song sung:
on and off-key
       Looking at the stained glass
The *Aron Hakodesh* and *Ner Tamid*

I told her not to sing
And she does

She told me not to say Kaddish
And so I don't

My mom learned to cook from superstitious women
I know the Kaddish they told her not to say

as if uttering the words of memory
isn't kosher

we don't say Kaddish in full

But we do say a few words

To share in the memory
And distrust in our memories

        so we can sift through photo albums and
children can reinterpret recipes with the same rolling pin

doubting memory is a way of pleasantness

and when we capture memories
        their paths are prayers of peace

Barbara

LEAH FLEISCHER

Lemon Steam

SEQUOIA HACK

The house smelled like Grandma's kitchen when Mama woke me up on Saturday morning. For a moment I thought Grandma had come back, but when I opened my eyes I saw Mama leaning over my bed. This was to be the first time that Mama and I made lemon curd after Grandma left, with Mama wearing Grandma's apron. Neither Mama nor I was ever allowed to wear that apron until now because Grandma claimed it was the one thing that made her curd *hers* and no one else's.

The apron had a pocket on the left breast, but because the pocket was sewn shut on all sides, Mama hadn't seen it before Saturday. She found the pocket while repairing a hole that had been ripped open by Grandma's rings as she had dried her hands with the apron. Mama had run her hands along the apron while sewing the hole shut and discovered a crease in the fabric a couple inches to the left of the hole—seemingly a mere seam under her palm—but Mama traced the border around all four sides of the pocket and felt a piece of paper under the fabric. When she ripped the stitches, she discovered Grandma's recipe for her lemon curd.

Grandma used to have a Meyer lemon tree in her front yard when she was still here. The tree produced lemons that resembled limes for eleven months of the year, only switching to a juicy yellow during the twelfth month. One hot, rainy Monday a year or so back, Mama picked me up from school and drove us to Grandma's house to help her juice lemons and sift sugar. I came to know this day to be the last time that I walked through Grandma's hibiscus and plumeria garden and through her door, where there was no rain.

I remember entering her kitchen, where we were immediately stopped by a cloud of lemon. Grandma emerged from the fragrant haze and lifted me off the ground with her tart, sticky hands. After she spun me around, she kissed my mother like butterflies, their eyelash "wings" flitting up and down, grazing each other's cheeks. I grabbed a spoon off of the silverware rack and dipped it into the bowl resting over a simmering pot of water. I could hardly reach the top of the bowl, let alone see what was inside, but I knew that once the spoon came out of the bowl, Grandma's lemon curd would be my butterfly kiss.

Her curd was glossy and golden from egg yolks; thick as the mist through which butterflies learn to fly, with a taste like the nectar that they drink from sweet rain forest flowers.

No matter how many times we tried to recreate the curd when Grandma was gone, the resulting consistency would resemble either rubbery Jell-O or runny lemon syrup. We never achieved the silky mousseline of Grandma's spread until now, when Mama found the hidden apron pocket with the lemon curd recipe inside.

The recipe Mama found was laminated in packing tape and sticky with dried lemon curd from years of use. Stapled to the paper was a small bag filled with glimmering powder. The recipe read as follows:

Lemon Curd

2 teaspoons lemon oil
½ teaspoon lemon pepper
2 cups lemonade
1½ cups lemon juice
5 teaspoons lemon balm
2¾ cups white sugar
10 tablespoons salted butter
6 large eggs
2 additional egg yolks
5 teaspoons powdered
    butterfly wing scales

1. Whisk lemon ingredients together in a bowl over a pot of bubbling water.

2. Add butter and sugar. Once the mixture has thickened, add eggs.

3. When the mixture becomes fragrant, remove from heat and stir in egg yolks. The heat remaining from the warm mixture will cook the additional egg.

4. Sprinkle top with scales and let them dissolve.

On the twelfth day of the twelfth month of two thousand and twelve, the curd that Mama and I made with Grandma's recipe formed into the exact lemon curd that I remember scooping from her bowl. We made many batches of it throughout that day, throughout that week, and throughout that month. Mama and I believed that making the curd would transport Grandma home from wherever she was in the world. We hoped she would walk through a forest of coconut trees with a crown of bougainvillea or emerge from a shallow stream and through our front door to give us butterfly kisses.

We ate the curd on toast, on crumpets, on scones, and over ice cream. I ate a spoonful a day, and I washed my face with it. I read *Plumbing for Dummies*, and Mama helped me detach the water main so we could fill the bathroom pipes with lemon curd. Eventually, I showered in lemon and washed my hands with lemon and bathed in it once a week. It was as if I was back with Grandma, perched on her knee stirring curd, immersed in lemony nirvana.

One day, I went into the bathroom to bathe in the lemon. In the tub, butterflies fluttered their new wings, admiring their own colors. My dress, colored with flowers from the tropics, fell off my shoulders as I stepped into the tub. The butterflies extracted the dress's spreading pigment with their proboscises. I turned the shower knobs as far left as they could go without falling off, and I deepened myself in the curd, submerging myself in a citrusy trance.

In this mist of juice and zest, butterflies rejoiced. They flew about the bathroom canopy, where the ceiling light promoted passion and warmth. Under the canopy was the understory of the rainforest where steam and lemony curd mingled. Monarchs and blue morphos drank from guavas and pineapples that hung from the shower curtain. At the rainforest bottom, bathroom tiles were covered in lemon curd. A Papilio demoleus, or what Mama calls a "lemon butterfly," with spots and stripes of black, green, and yellow, landed on my sticky shoulder. This Papilio demoleus flitted to the tip of my nose and batted its wings against my lashes. It was Grandma, with her citrusy butterfly kisses, arriving home from her travels.

CHAPTER TWO

When We Were Small

And the monsters under your bed grow up too.
With some of them,
You make friends.

FROM "INNOCENT," BY GAVI KLEIN

We remember the early years of our lives in fragments. The rest we fill in secondhand. Some memories deepen, others disappear. We trace scarred knees and remember the playground. We open an album of photos and remember that our bones are still growing. Sometimes these bones don't seem strong enough to bear the weight of the world, and sometimes they're much stronger than we imagined.

As we sift through our memories, we find there are parts of ourselves we want to cling to and parts we seek to escape, sometimes both at once. And so we move from childhood to adulthood, learning to inhabit our bodies, redraw boundaries, and recognize our strengths—stumbling and finding our balance again.

In an idealized childhood, there are **No Worries**.

Growing Up Girl captures the moment we're labeled by gender at birth, and how this moment shapes the rest of our lives.

As we face the uncertainties of growing up, we leave our **Innocent** selves behind.

In **Almost Thirteen & Seventeen**, Jewish identities and social forces clash.

Floating on water, a parent and child share a moment of **Serenity**.

The Things I Should Have Said winds through aquariums, road trips, and our changing relationships with our families.

A photographer examines the damaging **Labels** placed on us.

In **How to Label Yourself**, the writer unspools a thread of longing backward to her earliest memories.

The Game is an intimate snapshot of new love.

Love, creativity, and the awakening of the romantic self meet in **tuesday night on a street corner**.

We look past the schoolyard and into adulthood in **Here Lie Our Bones**.

In **You Bloom in the Art of Others**, the writer grapples with the loss of a childhood friend.

No Worries

TALI FEEN

Growing Up Girl

MAYA RABINOWITZ

It is the first thing they say when we come blinking into the world. Before we smell our mothers and before we are given a name—"It's a girl!" the doctor says. It is the earliest, most primitive definition. It is derived from nothing more than what lies between a baby's legs. From there, the parents sigh, or laugh, or sob with happiness, as if this was the news they'd been dreaming of, as if it had to be a girl, of course, and they forget that they would've been thrilled with a boy, too, for hadn't they told all their friends just days before that they didn't care, that all they wanted was a healthy baby?

The hospital is glad to have given this new life its first definition. The baby is whisked away and cleaned and then put in a clear plastic box with a soft pink hat and a soft pink blanket, and rolled into a row of other pink babies. "It's a girl!" read the signs that hang on the fronts of their boxes. The babies are born nearly blind, and they cannot see the color of their blankets, nor would they care if they could. Pink has no significance to them; it is the inside of their mothers, it is the tips of their fingers. It is for the comfort of the rest of the world that they are assigned a color. A soft, innocent, unprovocative color.

Being a girl is not something to think about. They say it is less important and less changeable than the color of your hair. The doctor makes the first definition, but don't worry, the world will fill in the rest before you know it.

There is girl clothing. If you are a girl, you are allowed to wear dresses and skirts. If you wear pants, your shirt better have a flower on it, or maybe some hearts and a kitten. This clothing is exclusive to girls.

One time, a little boy wore a dress to school. He was four years old, and it was an accepting school, so nobody laughed, but everybody stared. "It's because he has two moms," people said. "A dad would never let his son out in public looking like that." Some kids asked (as little kids do) why he wore girls' clothing. He said it was because flower hair clips were beautiful and fluffy, and bright skirts made him feel free. "I'm not a girl," he said. "I'm a person. I'm just me."

***

There are girl colors. Girls can wear pink and purple, and yellow, too. They can wear blue jeans sometimes, especially if there is something feminine—like a heart or a butterfly—stitched onto them. Before I was born, my parents refused to learn my gender. Family members and friends were desperate to know. "How do we know what color clothing to buy?" they asked. "You are not letting us define your baby." My mothers were proud that they had held off the world for just a few months longer. All they wanted was a healthy baby, and it irritated them that the societal gender craze had already slipped through the cracks of their home, reaching for an unborn life. My mothers told their family and friends to get over it, or to buy yellow and green if putting a girl in blue was such an atrocity. "It's because the baby has two moms," they'd say. "A straight woman would put her daughter in pink."

There are specific ways that girls should act. One time, a little girl went to summer camp. Everybody thought she was a boy, because she wore shirts with trucks and little cargo shorts every day, even into the pool. She had short hair and crooked teeth and brilliant blue eyes, and she would growl at anyone who looked her way. She was six years old, and it was an accepting camp in a progressive neighborhood, so nobody laughed, but some kids pointed. When the children lined up to get on the buses to the swimming pool, people wondered why she was in line to get on the girls' bus. (Now I wonder why they even *had* a girls' bus.) Two children teased her one day. "You're a boy," they said. "NO!" she shouted. "I'm a girl. I'm a girl because I say so."

Most girls grow into women. The world does not like this. Women have brains and hips, and they can stand up for themselves. The world prefers girls. When they are born, they are dressed in soft pink, because biologically, pink softens the temper of enemies. Girls are well-behaved and kind. It is easier to not hate a girl than it is to not hate a woman. So the world pushes its women back in time. "Be hairless," it says. "Be coveted, be untouchable." A girl is a symbol of beauty that women wax and pluck and burn and dumb themselves down into. A girl is a vessel that must be prepared to someday hold a baby. Give her dolls and toy houses and pretend veils for pretend weddings; she needs to start practicing now. Get it through her head that this is what she wants to be.

Once, a girl almost watched herself take a powerful country in hand, in the highest seat of power. For one second, the definitions that the world had placed around her neck began to lighten. Ha, said the world, just kidding. Try again later. Maybe next time, it will be different. Maybe next time, I will take a woman as she is, nasty or ugly or smart or bold. Try again later, says the world. Maybe tomorrow, I will define a woman as whoever she wants to be.

Innocent

GAVI KLEIN

Little girls in bright white dresses.
Little girls in bright white dresses with orange juice stains on them,
And little plastic plates covered in painted yellow flowers
Under half-slices of homemade pizza because
Little stomachs only need halves.

Monsters under your bed and bigger hands around yours
Fancy shoes that are not your own and sticks of loud red lipstick
    that look nice
On quiet pastel walls.
Beauty lies in so many places that older eyes can't seem to see and
The world is something at your fingertips that you have yet to discover
    how to hold.

Then the world is shrinking around you,
And you are shooting upward,
And the monsters under your bed grow up too.
With some of them,
You make friends.

One day, suddenly, you can see clearly,
(Or perhaps you were seeing clearly before)
But either way, now you know
That we don't last forever,
And sometimes our not-forevers
Are still shorter than we were promised.
You learn through mistakes,
That *no* doesn't really mean *no*,
And *yes* doesn't mean what it promises either,
And people don't always laugh because it's funny,
They laugh because you are laughing,
And that despite words like *love*,
There will always be moments when you are alone.

You are piled on with tales,
Of times and places and people that you never knew, but somehow,
Still shape everything that you are.
You are
Handed something like wisdom that you are not sure you want to have,
Taught that x is right and y is wrong,
And God forbid you question that,
But
God forbid you don't.

The monsters under your bed are real, you see,
But there is nothing you can do for them,
And there is nothing they can do for you.

They used to be your friends,
Maybe they still are.
You learn that sometimes it is difficult to tell the difference between a
    good thing
And a safe thing.
You learn that loss is more often invisible than it is not,
And that change sometimes means good things must go away.

You buy a gun for the monsters who have taken to sleeping in your bed.

They look into your eyes,
And smile a smile painfully familiar.
They reach out a hand,
To comfort you, maybe,
And you pull the trigger.

The glass stings as it rains down.

Little hands, little feet, little hearts.
Why do little things always seem to die a little
When they grow bigger?

Almost Thirteen & Seventeen

AUDREY HONIG

Almost Thirteen

An adult in the eyes of the community.
But what does this mean?

I look around at these eyes after my speech, quietly.
My parents' eyes are nervous and beaming.

The boys from school squint their eyes and giggle
At the funny Jewish hats.

I enter adulthood with Torah and tradition,
And celebrate with the hugging game and the Cha-Cha Slide.

Monday, I enter back into the halls of seventh grade,
Where I hear that someone kissed this weekend.

I remember that I am a "Daughter of the Commandment" now.
Ready to take on the full *mitzvot*, the world.

But at school, I am asked,
Can you go to heaven if you don't believe in Jesus?

Seventeen

At the end of eighth grade, a boy wrote in his yearbook:
"Audrey Honig: Concentration Camp."

This was during our Holocaust unit in history class,
Yet he made this joke.

Weeks later, other boys were banging on our door,
Yelling *dreidel, dreidel, dreidel* at my dad.

He recalled how he taught them that word
In a kindergarten show-and-tell during Hanukkah.

How could they not know that "Jew" is not an insult?
Not a punchline to a joke. Not a burden.

Today I am proud of everything "Jewish" can mean,
Whether it's celebrating a holiday,
Being kind to myself,
Or passing the love of Hebrew on.

I love who I am. I love who I am.

Serenity

AIDYN LEVIN

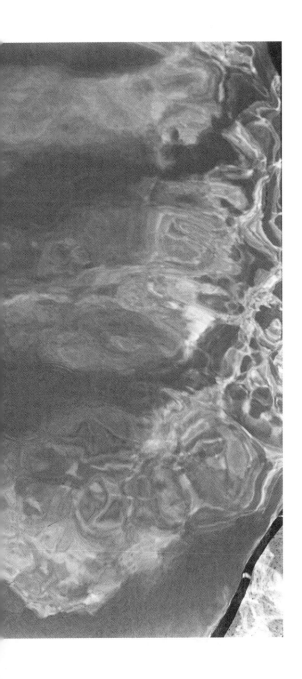

The Things I Should Have Said

MAKEDA ZABOT-HALL

I should have said I never enjoyed the aquarium in the third grade
that it made me uneasy when I thought of
all the sad sea animals that longed to be set free
and I should have said I missed my mom
when my parents would ship me off
to spend the summer with my grandparents
I missed my mom
and I should have said that
and I should have said at the age of fourteen I no longer
enjoyed the company of the boys
at the lunch table
and that I wanted to be alone
because I felt alone
and I should have said
that when my siblings went on road trips with my father
that I wanted to come
but I felt paralyzed
by the fear of the small red car closing in on me
and I should have said on my fifteenth birthday
that I'm no longer a child
and I wanted to experience life raw and full
without my parents looking over my shoulder
and when I woke up in the middle of the night
and my mom asked me if everything was alright
I should have told her I was scared
I should have told my mom I wasn't okay
and that I couldn't sleep
and that I wanted the days to end
as soon as they started
and that I missed the fish
and being fourteen
and the little red car
I should have told my mom I was scared of being sixteen
and that life seemed like a black hole that was
suffocating me alive

these are the things I should have said
these are the things I wanted to say
these are the things I should have said, but didn't

Labels

ANNIE POOLE

How to Label Yourself

ABIGAIL FISHER

2018. Your history class learns about the Stonewall Riots. Pretend you've never heard of them. Ask enough questions to show you've never done private research on the subject, but not enough to make someone think you'd want to. Someone will tell you that the allies always turn out queer. Having known for years now, you will blush defiantly. You will remove the rainbow pin from your messenger bag.

2017. Start to listen to music that would make others want to share head-phones with you. Make Fiona Apple the background track to your high school career. Wonder what it must be like to bite into her last name. Does the juice drip down your chin? Imagine her lips taste like a Granny Smith apple, and the phantom tartness will make you pucker your lips.

2016. Go to summer camp and meet a girl from Pakistan with a smile like a chipped teacup. Go back home and describe it to your friend, who will say that if "you love her so much you should marry her." Laugh and talk about the boy in the blue Nike T-shirt whom you say you want to kiss.

2015. In chemistry, learn about polar opposites. Let the knowledge damn near rip you in half. Remember the word *bipolar* and know that you may at least be caught between two nameable extremes. Decide you don't need labels. Pretend to be an open book and stop hoping someone finds your diary.

2014. Write a story about a twin you never had. Your twin wears dark eye-liner and combat boots. She likes picking her cuticles until they're not red but purple. Try to summon her in a séance. Leave the story untitled by accident.

2013. Stop getting your period. Name your future children. Soleil. Kochava. Rivaya Eylah. Emily Rose.
  Your English class talks about suicide as an act of self-love.

2012. Fall in love with anomia. You're so used to having the words to describe things that it's a relief to stop naming what you see. When you learn the word for the inability to name things, cry deep and long. Remember the taste of your best friend's thumb against your chapped lips.

Write a poem about secrets that rhymes.

2011. Get your period for the first time. Ask your dad to buy tampons even though your mom is home. Tell him you like the kind that he got even though they sting and you don't know how to use them. Tell all your friends about your initiation into womanhood and end friendships when they spread the word.

2010. Keep a diary and hope somebody finds it. Always use first and last names so that the person who does find it will know exactly who's responsible for the way you turned out.

2009. Play games with your best friend where you take turns being the boyfriend and pretend to make out with each other by covering your mouths with your thumbs. It looks so real that it almost feels real. Lock the door and pretend it's because you're playing a game that involves costume changes. On playdates with other people, look at her then look away so you don't seem overeager. Secretly hope that the other friends leave so you can play your game.

2008. Start believing in premonitions. Intuit that your mom's friend will bring her a T-shirt with *Obama* spelled out in Hebrew letters. When she opens her gift and finds exactly what you suspected, remind your parents that you knew it all along. When they accuse you of peeking, blush defiantly. Sit at the grown-ups' table and sulk. Your mom's friend teaches at Columbia, and her wife teaches at Barnard. Pretend you aren't listening when they whisper sweetly to each other.

2007. Discover your ability to hear the basement from the attic and practice naming the things you hear. When you hear nothing but dishes clattering, call that love.

2006. Let your grandmother buy you a dress. Relish being her Beautiful Girl. Ask her for her lipstick and let her brush your hair.

2005. Fall in love with bedtime stories. Don't let them transport you, but let them help you name what you see. Let their neat endings tuck you in at night. Get used to the smell of your mom's perfume and the way your dad's voice drops off while he's fighting off sleep to give you a proper good night. Wonder what other people's dads sound like when they're tired.

Dream about a bedtime story that never ends.

2004. Maxwell from your "Music Together" class kisses you on the lips. You don't remember feeling it despite the photographic evidence.

2003. Learn to talk. Let your first word be "me." Your mother will hear it as "ma."

2002. Experience a world as bright as a freezer or a hospital room. Learn to recognize smells and tastes. Curl your tongue in a tremendous effort to form words. Your mother will see her own curled tongue and feel secure in the fact that you are hers.

2001. Let the doctor wrap you in a pink blanket. Scratch the hospital bracelet the nurse tightened around your wrist. Don't tug at the label that fits, and brace yourself for the ones that won't.

The Game

JULIET NORMAN

I swear your eyes were a candlelight
flickering toward my own personal oceans
and every piece of matter around us dribbled down to dust
because the things I'd been looking forward to
were not nearly
as stimulating as the game you and I shared that day
and every other class period just like it
the ever so addictive routine of our eyes
doing more than just seeing but feeling
all the way across the room
playing at the divertissement of who could glimpse
the other without getting caught
And so far, we were both losing

tuesday night on a street corner

ALEXA HULSE

i don't think she knows,
but she is the one who taught me what love is.
it was tuesday night
on a street corner
and we were a sleepy kind of silly,
which is the best way to be
when you're young and just beginning.
the winter air flushed her cheeks with merlot hues
and i had never seen anything quite as beautiful.

she took my hands and put them in the pockets of her pea coat,
traced her lavender fingernails along the creases in my palm,
found valleys and mountains within me that i had never taken the
    time to explore.
i know she is made up of the same elements as me,
but her touch turned my stomach into an elementary school science
    fair project,
a volcano made at the kitchen table out of clay and vinegar and baking
    soda,
only one chemical reaction away from bubbling over.

it took everything in me to work up the courage to kiss her.
as we stood on the street corner
that was familiar to her and foreign to me
i finally pressed my lips to hers.
i tasted clementines and tobacco and warmth,
no overpriced lip balm or pastry from the coffee house around the
    corner could ever be as sweet.
that kiss made me want to paint again.
i wanted to capture the gap that glowed in the middle of her crescent
    moon smile
and the way her eyes creased when i gave her a copy of my favorite
    book.
i wanted to use the brushes i had just gotten for hanukkah and my best
    oil paints:
pink for me,

purple for her,
the whole color palette for both of us.

rainbows dripped from her lips when she told me she loved me
and i had never seen anything quite as beautiful.

Here Lie Our Bones

MAYA SAVIN MILLER

when we were small
we traced these bones
for the slightest hint of wounding
scars as pedestrian as skinned knees
as desired as a burst pomegranate
we compared knuckles and kneecaps
like we were two cracked honeysuckles

All this before we knew about fault lines
Before we knew what it meant
To breathe with hands around the neck
How to bury the dead in the schoolyard
How a spine can carry a bullet
Like a stone through glass
And suddenly there's a backslash
Running through this playground

Peel back the scab like
Sunrise over a bird shot in flight
Find your bones cracked from weight
Like a father asleep
Under the carriage of a train

can't you see?
some wounds cannot be
collected like bodies
for your burial ground
so I say
throw these bones skyward
and call them beautiful

You Bloom in the Art of Others

SHOSHANA MANISCALCO

Auditorium

On a frozen March night during my junior year of high school, my mother drags me to a lecture about drugs and the teenage brain. It is meant for parents, and I am one of the only students there. I listen to a middle-aged woman drone on about how marijuana is a gateway drug. I'm convinced that she's never actually talked to a teenager in her life. Anger boils inside me. I can't believe that my school waited until now to start conversations about drug abuse. It is too late.

Best Friend

At the start of second grade, a very shy new girl in my class introduces herself to me. Her name is Lily. Within a few days, we become best friends, mostly because neither of us is particularly talkative in class, but at home, we never stop talking. We plan our dream jobs (I want to be a doctor, she wants to be an artist), and our dream houses, and our dream families, and we do not stop dreaming.

Counselors

On a dark Monday morning in February, every school counselor in the city is sent to our school. A few of them come into my first-period class. One sits at what should be her desk and reassures us that we will be okay. I storm out of the room in anger, except I don't leave my seat at all. I do not say a word. Maybe ignoring them will make them disappear. How can they be so confident that things will be okay if my ex-best friend is dead? I hate that she will always be my ex-best friend now.

Drug

(noun): Something that causes addiction, habituation, or a marked change in consciousness. Examples: caffeine, marijuana, alcohol, *heroin*, thinking about you so often hoping it will bring you back.

Epidemic

They warn us frequently about going out. Even though we live in suburbia, everything trickles down from the city. They tell us the city is flooded with drugs. We should not talk to strangers because they might try to sell us some. They tell us to run away and find an adult. They forget to mention it's usually not the strange men we see in the city. Instead, it is our co-workers, our friends, people we trust. Sixteen people in my nice, safe suburb died from opioids in 2016. At sixteen, she was the youngest.

February

My parents go to Torah study at the synagogue every Saturday morning. Today, as the clock slowly approaches noon, I wonder why my parents aren't home yet. Something feels wrong. Moments later, the garage door opens, and my mother calls for me. "Shoshana, could you please come here?" There is something eerie in her tone, but I cannot pinpoint what it is. My head starts to spin with all the horrible possibilities as I walk down the hallway to the stairs. Before I can even make it to the bottom, she tells me that Lily passed away last night. I want to scream and cry, but my throat has forgotten how to form sounds, and my tear ducts are suddenly empty. Ever since that day, February has always felt like the longest month, and I hate it.

Giggling

When we were little, Lily and I made up our own games. The people at school didn't understand us, but we could understand each other without even speaking. In one of our games, we squatted as low to the ground as possible, waddled around, and yelled "Hamburger!" in funny accents until we fell to the floor in laughter.

Haunted

Her funeral is on Valentine's Day, a day we always agreed was dumb. The rabbi stands with his guitar in front of countless displays of her art and encourages us to sing. Silence.

Ignore

We don't talk for two years because of one boy. Two weeks into the spring semester of our junior year, I finally decide to make amends with her on Monday. But for her, Monday never comes.

Junior Year

Everyone says junior year is the hardest part of high school, but I'm pretty sure no one accounted for your ex-best friend dying.

Kiss

She blacked out that cold November night at the school dance. We were fourteen, and she was drunk on stolen tequila and high on tranquilizers. We were fourteen, and my friends made me watch her—so they didn't have to—to make sure she didn't do anything dumb, like pulling the lighter she kept in her bra on any guys (which she did about three times while my back was turned). We were fourteen, and she fell asleep on my crush's shoulder that night. With Lily passed out between us, he and I held hands while waiting for our parents. Six months later, she tried to use that night against me, claiming she kissed him, trying to get me to stop talking to him because she thought he was bad for me. We were fourteen, and I stopped talking to her forever.

Last Words

I do not, cannot, believe that Lily is dead when I hear the news. To prove to myself my mother was wrong, I scour social media. She posted on Twitter fifteen hours ago, so maybe that is a sign. The tweet reads, "I'm fine <3." How could she lie to me like that? How could she be fine last night but dead this morning?

Mourning

For weeks after her death, it felt like all the light in the world had vanished. I was drunk on guilt and shame, stuck in a downward spiral of what-ifs. I cried for days on end, only stopping when my family was around. When a tear escaped my eye at dinner a week after the funeral, my mother was quick to scold me. "I was close to her too, Shoshana! But you don't see me crying about it weeks later!" My stomach felt heavy, full of shame for not simply getting over it. At that moment, I chose to stop mourning her death. Enough was enough. I locked the remaining grief deep inside of myself, so no one could tell I was hurt. I saved those feelings for poetry no one would read. I stopped talking about her completely.

Name

In English, Shoshana means "rose" or "lily." As kids, we joked about having the same name. I see now that the similarities stretched beyond just our names. We both suffered immensely. We picked each other up when we hit rock bottom, talked each other down off of high ledges. We became the help we needed for each other.

Optimism

As the dreadful winter finally thaws, in the first few breaths of spring, I watch as the roses begin to bloom. I wait...and wait...and wait...until one summer day when the air is much too warm. Sweat drips down my forehead as a beautiful white flower catches my eye. The lilies in my garden are finally in bloom. Stretching from the depths of the dirt out into the light. Reaching for the warm sunshine. Maybe we are going to be okay after all.

Possibility

What if we never got into that fight? Would we still have been friends during sophomore and junior years of high school? Better yet, what if I forgave her more than a week before she died? Would I still be carrying this regret in my pocket? What if I knew about her drug addiction? Could I have done anything to help her? What if she told her mom she needed help sooner than hours before she died? Would she still be here? If she didn't die, would I have ever forgiven her? Can I even say that I have?

Quiet

The

    falling

        snow

           is both

               too quiet

                  and

                    too loud.

Refraction

She saw the world through shades of blue, through the lens of her camera. She had a skill for capturing the complexity of emotions, while barely feeling any at all. One day, she dressed me in shades of gray, painted my face with makeup, and took me out into the snow to take photos. Our mothers sat in my bright kitchen and sipped tea as they called out to us to put on coats. Lily kept her camera tinted blue, exaggerating the fluffy snow falling around us, and the sadness in both of our hearts. I changed my camera settings too. The blue is more expressive; all the stories I tried to tell are sad. I didn't change the settings back for years.

Sushi

On the second day of second grade, we play a name game. Going around the room, we each say our name and what item we are bringing to a picnic that starts with the same letter. I am stumped and suddenly forget every word I know that starts with "S." Lily suggests that I bring sushi. Everyone in the class, except for Lily and me, either doesn't like sushi or has never tried it. Soon enough, the whole class calls me Sushi more often than my own name. It follows me like a shadow until high school. Now it is the only thing I cannot stand to be called.

Time

Healing is not linear. In my head, I go back in time and search for warning signs from Lily. I pretend I could have done something to stop this all from happening, despite the fact that I had no idea what she was going through and no intention of finding out. I want nothing more than to feel whole, for the gaping wound in my chest to close. Weeks go by, and I don't think about her. Months later, I find pictures of us from a party when we were fourteen. She was sitting on my bed, long brown hair covering one of her eyes, as she focused on her red BIC lighter. Her finger hovered less than a centimeter above the flame. She knew if she got any closer, it surely would burn her, but she loved to test her limits. How silly I must look now, screaming at my dead friend through my laptop about how she never should have taken those drugs. Supposedly, time heals all wounds, except I'm not sure I ever want this one to close.

Uncertainty

This story is as much about me as it is about her, so why do I feel like it's not mine to tell?

Vulnerability

I do not remember the first time I told someone about Lily. I only remember several terrifying moments trying to explain how hard it is to feel so alone and so helpless while trying to not be met with pity. In college, I begin to accept that I cannot keep this piece of me in the pile of junk beneath my bed. Acceptance feels like coming home.

Writing

It has taken years to be okay enough to write about you, Lily. I still see you in spring when the flowers bloom, a rebirth after the dark and cold. In life, you bloomed in making art out of your sadness. In death, you bloom in the art of others. I still see you when the snowflakes are heavy, and the world looks like a snow globe. And it reminds me of when snow was just snow, not a reminder of what could have been.

X

…As in gone

…As in unknown

…As in unfinished

…As in no address to send this to

You

You would not want me to be sad. So instead, Lily, I'm picking up the shattered pieces of my heart and creating a mosaic in your name.

Zichronah Livrachah (May her memory be for a blessing)

Every week at services, when we come to the prayer for those we have lost, it is customary to say the name of someone only on the anniversary of their death. I say your name every week, Lily. My heart cannot bear for you to be erased, for my lips to forget the feeling of your name, for my eyes to forget the softness in your smile. I cannot forget you the way you thought you would be forgotten. As long as I live, I will carry you in my heart. I am not ready to move on, but I am ready for both of us to finally be free.

CHAPTER THREE

A Healthy Collection of Hardships and Blessings

I try to understand this confined brain
Waiting for it to untangle

FROM "BRAIN ON LIFE," BY CECELIA ROSS

Sensory experiences of all kinds—a welcome hug, wind in our hair as we ride a bike, shaky hands during a performance—reverberate through our bodies and become embedded in our minds, shaping who we are and how we feel. Likewise, our emotions manifest physically: when we are distressed, we toss and turn; when we feel joy, we laugh or dance.

But while our bodies and minds feel integrated in some moments, they are disconnected in others. We might feel emotionally strong when our bodies are worn out, or physically liberated when our minds don't feel free. As we move through the world, we carry the burden of all kinds of expectations, making it hard for us to be fully ourselves.

In the midst of this struggle, our relationships, traditions, and creativity bring us comfort. We express ourselves through art forms we've studied from a young age and ones we'll never master. And we push back against the systems that fragment us, asserting our right to be whole.

Melting Head 34 refracts the body and captures the swirling chaos of the mind.

In **Brain on Life**, the speaker reckons with the patterns holding her back.

The Right Words can give us power over our emotions.

Too often, the weight of expectations can make us feel like we're **Drowning**.

The Shape of Beauty: Reflections on an Adolescent Eating Disorder explores how self-criticism can invade our minds and become dangerous to our bodies.

An artist represents the unsettling nature of **Anxiety**.

The Menu is Overwhelming, full of challenge and possibility.

Social expectations and monsters fight one another inside the mind of **Pigtails Girl**.

Nature emerges from behind sharp corners, re-grounding us, in **Soft and Hard**.

A Letter to My Past Self: what would you say to yourself if you could go back in time?

With a varied color palette, **Me, Myself, and I** reminds us that we are multifaceted.

In **Fairy Poem**, we are absorbed into a world of fantastical indulgence.

Just thinking of another person can bring us warmth, as in **Sparks**.

Free Woman reminds us that life can be joyful when we are our full selves.

Melting Head 34

ELIANA SHAPERE

Brain on Life

CECELIA ROSS

I try to understand this confined brain
Waiting for it to untangle
Desperate to hold even a minute
To strip away the plastered souls I've designed

Apprehension, Embarrassment, Disquiet
They're who built this deceiving pond
Leaving me behind
An icy pool of desperation
I never knew was there

My joy collapses in bright light
While I pretend I haven't
Exiled myself, drifting away
Into an act of content solitude

I sat in the car
And I promised myself
As I watched the street lights
Through the raindrops
I'll make it stop

But I never escaped
Waiting an eternity
For myself to emerge

They say there's still hope
That I'm so young
"Time is on your side"
But I can't help asking
Is that true?

The Right Words

ABIGAEL GOOD

You don't know when the anxiety started. You remember a dream, a corridor of locked doors, a key that won't work, a metal block in your stomach, waking up and pacing your bedroom floor—eight years old? Nine? Older? But you're not even sure there can be a solid starting point for something like this, one event you can mark as the first time.

You're older now. You keep track in your journal. Nebulous notes, without labels—though you've tried labels before, sure. One book you read in seventh grade made you give this terrible feeling a name: anxiety. But you rejected that eventually, as you did every other label. No word ever fit. This feeling was surely too trivial to merit any of those sharp-edged words that belonged to psychiatrists and mental health lecturers.

And yet, you always knew that it hurt too much to be nothing. You knew you should say something. You just couldn't find the right words. My stomach hurts, you'd say. I just don't feel good.

That changed one winter. It was a snow day. You slept over at a friend's house, woke up shaky. You felt sick. It was that feeling, reawakened a few weeks before by a gruesome murder scene in some show. You'd thought you'd successfully distracted yourself from it, that it had retreated from the battlefield of your mind for another few months. But this morning it was back hard, for no reason. No trigger, just a blast. It chased you outside to the freezing air, where you paced and tried to breathe.

You apologized to your friend and went home. You thought you'd feel safer there. Instead you felt trapped.

For years you had kept how bad this feeling got a secret, as if denying it a name made it powerless. That morning, breathing was so hard and your limbs so shaky that you couldn't sit still. You told your mom you wanted to see a doctor. You wanted to see a therapist. For years you had wanted nothing less. It was so bad that morning that every other fear fled. All you were scared of anymore was this feeling.

But it was a snow day. All offices were closed. The one time you could bring yourself to ask for help, help was not taking appointments.

You stood in the icy air and looked out at a storm worse than any you had weathered before.

That day you threw up a few times. Drifted back and forth between "mostly okay" and "shaking with anxiety." You barely slept. The night was endless pilgrimages between the bed you couldn't bear to lie in and the bathroom where you shook and waited to throw up again, sucked on an ice cube in your dry mouth, stared at yourself in the mirror. The next day didn't get better. Power outages kept offices closed. You ate only a few bites throughout the day—you never could eat when you felt like this. You stopped activities you'd barely started because nothing took your mind away. You just wanted to stop feeling.

The episode faded slowly. You missed a day of school after panicking in the hallway. Doctor's offices opened. You remembered how to breathe.

The records in your journal have sharp-edged words now. Anxiety. Therapist. Medication. But they are so much lighter than that metal box in your stomach. The hallway of doors doesn't look so long. It makes you think, sometimes, that giving it a name made you more powerful instead.

Drowning

ALEX BERMAN

The Shape of Beauty
Reflections on an Adolescent Eating Disorder

AHAVA HELFENBAUM

I remember standing on the scale in front of the mirror, trying on my uniform kilt. It was a blue, yellow, and green hunk of tough cloth strewn with pencil marks and holes. Its imperfections were a map of four years of school, and my four-year transition from grade four to grade seven.

I looked into the mirror and sucked in, depriving my torso of air in an attempt to button the last faded skirt button around my protruding waist bone. The same button that had not moved an inch since grade four, and which I refused to move because it would mean I was fat and worthless.

The scale's dark screen whirred mechanically, calculating my worth. I grimaced because I was a pound heavier than last week. It must have been the rice cakes I gorged on at midnight. I knew I shouldn't have done it, but I didn't want my stomach to make noises in class again like it did the day before; it was too mortifying. Then I realized that if I stopped eating granola in my yogurt, I wouldn't have any carbs at lunch at all.

I glanced at the nail scissors behind me on the shelf and thought about my shower the night before, the pieces of hair that had washed down the drain as I stared at my trembling hands. Then I woke from the haze of my daydream and instinctively grabbed my ponytail, feeling the jagged edges fresh from the trim. Because even in that state of delirium and exhaustion, I had to ensure that my hair was still enviable, that I was still beautiful.

I dragged my empty stomach down the hallway and into bed, the rest of my body following. There, I went through my nightly ritual of picturing myself in a form-fitting dress on the beach, laughing and smiling. I saw my hair shiny and nourished like it once was, my teeth white and pearly, my arms and fingers long and delicate, and most importantly, I saw myself skinny. I saw me, but beautiful. Only once I had done that would my brain be allowed to rest, and only then could I sleep.

For two years, I practiced this ritual every night.

Why? Why did I let my anorexia dictate my life? That's easy. Because "the fat" was an obstacle in my way.

One of the most noticeable things about me is that I am stubborn. As a child, I spent hours attempting to climb out of my crib. I would never cry, and I would never ask for help; I would simply address the bars of the crib as the obstacle and reaching the other side of the bars as the objective.

But the most fascinating part is that whenever I escaped my wooden prison after hours of determination, I simply crawled up to whichever parent had fallen asleep on the floor long ago and fell asleep beside them. I wanted to escape the crib because it was my objective, because it was my goal, not because I did not like the crib.

That is how I have chosen to understand my anorexia. When I was sick, I was a child determined to reach the world outside of the crib, to reach the realm of beauty because I thought it would grant me the freedom of being desirable. All that mattered was achieving beauty by eliminating any excess millimeter of fat. Ironically, this need imprisoned me, not freed me, until I convinced myself that all that mattered was that I become the shape of beautiful.

I lost my hair. I couldn't concentrate in class, and my grades dropped as a result. I cried so much during those years that my eyes were constantly red and sore.

Yet through it all, I kept up appearances. I brought eye drops to school to ensure no one would question my puffy eyes. I gave away all my snacks at school, only ate one yogurt for lunch, and ate a large dinner as my one meal at home so that my mom would never suspect anything. I had convinced my audience, but I was living two separate lives. And it was so lonely.

I have been healthy for years now, yet I still feel every twist and turn of the crazy roller coaster that was my journey to recovery. I remember the night I cut my hair in the shower for the first time, but I also remember the day, two years later, when I finally threw away that uniform skirt, determined to begin a new chapter in my life. By then, I did not care if I had to move the button or not. And I still don't.

And it's funny that even though I don't care what I weigh anymore, and I'm happy in my own skin, I still remember all of the smells, sounds, and textures from my past life. Like the heat of pride when my grade-four skirt finally fit perfectly on my grade-eight body, and the taste of that awful vanilla yogurt. The sound of my rumbling stomach, and the bitter coldness of the metal scale. I remember all these things because they have the distinct shape of what I thought was beauty, which I now know to be the shape of sadness.

Anxiety

AIDYN LEVIN

The Menu is Overwhelming

EMANUELLE SIPPY

Sometimes age is as muddled as life's unanswerable questions.

Arbitrary, in our cravings for adulthood and infancy.

Forget deciding—knowing alone is a task so cumbersome
that control is not envied but rather exiled.

When worry overpowers, I order life without
obligation,
nuance,
and choice.

But when fulfillment reaches its boil, life *with* makes my mouth water.

No, it's not a prix fixe.

Forget knowing—life *with* requires deciding.

Because
Orders rarely come as expected and
Orders, sometimes, don't come.

Pigtails Girl

ALEX BERMAN

Pigtails Girl sits down to lunch. She had noticed her friends whispering while she waited on the lunch line. Or maybe this was only thoughts hurricaning inside her head. She tightens her pigtails to make the thoughts stop. She reminds herself of her perfection. Her awards and good grades. Her popularity. Her mom's encouragement. She's golden and cannot be anything but. Pigtails Girl is a ray of sunshine in an otherwise bleak, empty world. Pigtails Girl is the apple of her mother's eye. Her teacher's pet. Her friends' confidante. She sang a song about the rain and everybody clapped. She is enchantingmanicsupernaturaldreamstargirl.

She feels a tap on her shoulder. A friend wants to ENGAGE IN CONVERSATION™. She turns and smiles, because when she was little her mother said, "If you make stupid faces they'll stick." Isabelle invites Pigtails Girl "to a sleepover tonight? Like, with just the four of us?"

Pigtails Girl accepts. "That sounds like sooo much fun!" Isabelle and the other girls exchange secret smiles. Pigtails Girl's hands inch up to her head.

"We were thinking…" Ivy's tongue flashes across her lips in a way that *Seventeen* would call "sexy and enticing." She's been practicing flirting and has developed a habit. She continues, biting her lip, "that we could give you a makeover!"

"Um, sure!"

Pigtails Girl remembers her last makeover. She was ten. She had just won her first of many academic awards. She stood, blinded by stage lights. Everyone clapped. She should have been overjoyed, but she couldn't focus. She thought about her grandmother, because she had heart problems and Pigtails Girl didn't want her to die and she hoped she would get a good grade on that recent math test because she needed to keep her average up did her hair look stupid? It did, didn't it. The voices had always been there. Pigtails Girl was told that everybody has voices, but most people's stopped when you told them to. Hers never did. They made her feet tap and her chest ache. They made her feel like she was always plugged into a socket, always ON. She wanted to claw her hair out of her scalp. She wanted to find the plug and rip it out of her chest. She wanted to squeeze her head still until she just. Stopped. Thinking. She hoarded rubber bands and hair ties and bows and ribbons and barbed wire—anything to tie back the monster that lived in her. She could feel its poison leaching through her veins, spreading and building, and so she tied off the passages, squeezing her thoughts like so many tender biceps awaiting shots, until her lips turned blue.

She wears pigtails to indicate her youth and naivete.

She wears pigtails to represent her bright spirit.

She wears pigtails because if she doesn't tie up her loose ends, she might explode: guts spewing out of her like confetti (SURPRISE! Pigtails Girl does NOT have her life together!).

She wears pigtails because she did yesterday and Pigtails Girl is resistant to change.

The people around her buy it hook, line, and sinker. They need her beautiful aura, her infectious positivity. They need to believe in her perfection. In an angel. She wraps them in hair ties and feeds them lies, because maybe someday she'll believe them too.

She's still waiting.

Pigtails Girl packs a bag and walks to Isabelle's apartment. She practices smiling in the elevator mirror. She is enchantingmanicsupernaturaldream-stargirl.

She knocks on Isabelle's door and hears the sound of six feet pounding down the hall. A stampede. Her friends open the door, enveloping her in hugs. Their voices surround her in a cacophony of elongated vowels.

She smiles and laughs and returns their wild calls. Their rituals are foreign and yet so familiar. She has read about these creatures, observed them in their natural habitat. She has laughed with them, telling secrets specially made for sharing in the dark. But she is not one of them.

Soon, it's time for them to begin FUN SLEEPOVER ACTIVITIES™. Pigtails Girl engages in nail painting, friendship-bracelet making, and Kiss Marry Kill (kiss Jack B, marry Theo, and kill Tyler). She giggles and gossips, playing her part. The girls have problems and Pigtails Girl fixes them. She assures Ivy that she totally looks hot, reminds Simona that her mom can't be mad forever, and promises Isabelle to help with her bio lab.

Finally, it is her turn to be saved. The others erase her face and draw her a new one. Her eyes are even more sparkly, her cheeks even more rosy. She is even more perfect, even more golden. She looks in the mirror and sees who she should be. She makes a mental note to buy highlighter.

The girls burrow into their sleeping bags, careful not to smudge freshly polished nails.

"Can we watch the movie now?" asks Ivy.

"In a minute," says Isabelle. She turns to Pigtails Girl. "How about we take out your pigtails?" Isabelle removes a curling iron from her makeup bag. "Your hair would look so good in curls."

"Or flat ironed!" says Simona. "Or you could cut it all off like that Parkland girl!"

"No!" Pigtails Girl clutches her pigtails. She tries to crawl away from her friends, but her legs are trapped in her sleeping bag.

"Calm down!" laughs Isabelle. "I was just joking."

Pigtails Girl turns away.

The girls lie across the carpet, their expressions emanating distaste.

"It's just that you've had those pigtails for so long!" says Simona.

"No, yeah, I know," says Pigtails Girl. "It's fine." The girls continue to stare. "Do you guys want to start the movie?"

"Sure!" says Simona, always eager to de-escalate conflict. Isabelle turns on the TV. They watch *Mean Girls*, which Pigtails Girl finds ironic. She laughs and she almost means it.

Eventually, they turn out the lights. Pigtails Girl strains to hear what her friends are whispering about, but can't. Eventually, she falls asleep to their murmurs.

Pigtails Girl wakes up to the sound of scissors above her head. She screams, then relaxes, realizing it is only Isabelle. "What are you doing?" Isabelle giggles behind Pigtails Girl, who turns to see Isabelle's greedy hands clutching her severed pigtails.

The elastics snap. In Pigtails Girl's imagination, the monster comes out screaming, erupting from Pigtails Girl's throat like a geyser. At first there is an empty wail. Then a torrent of fiery hail of biblical proportions. Rage spews from Pigtails Girl's pores. It festers and boils on the faces of her friends, leaving angry sores. Her lips return to a healthy red as the blood flows back to her. Her skin begins to split at the seams as she dives for her pigtails, dropped from Isabelle's hands in surprise. She cradles them to her chest and cries until she is just an empty skin sack.

In real life, Pigtails Girl walks home without a word.

So. Pigtails Girl is just Girl now. And Girl has nothing to hide.

Girl cuts off the rest of her hair while her mom is still at work. She shaves her head bald. She doesn't recognize herself in the mirror. She gets a razor cut and is surprised to see fresh, red, healthy blood dripping down her forehead. She had expected molten black sludge. It reaches her lips, and she tastes it. It doesn't taste like poison.

Lying on her bathroom floor is the monster, a mess of matted hair and ponytail holders. Its round dark eyes stare up at her sadly, and when she reaches down to touch it, her hand finds not solid flesh but cut hair and snapped rubber bands. She sweeps them aside, and all that is left are the monster's marble eyes.

Girl's mother comes home and finds Girl sitting on the couch. Girl's mom doesn't say anything. She just puts her arms around Girl, and Girl cries all the tears she didn't know she had. Girl knows there will be questions later, but right now she floods the house. The couch floats up and becomes an island. Just a girl and her mom. They are stranded, but Girl doesn't care. She knows that eventually everything floats back to shore.

For the rest of the weekend, Mom and Girl spend their time remembering what things were like when Girl was imperfect. When Girl was still just Girl like she is now. Mom asks Girl why she shaved her head, and Girl says it's because she doesn't want to be perfect. Mom says she doesn't have to be. Girl tells Mom about the voices in her head. She tells her about the electricity that surges through her veins and about how she has exploded and how she is okay now. Mom tells Girl that it is probably not over and that probably it never will be. Mom tells Girl to let the electricity flow through her instead of insulating it and stopping it up. Then maybe she won't have to explode again.

"But what if I do?" says Girl.

Mom says it will be alright. She'll help pick up the pieces.

Voices still follow Girl on her walk to school. It is obvious to most passersby that Girl isn't right in the head. She wears a bandage on her scalp. Passersby can imagine that this is where the crazy she was hiding all along finally crept out. They can't see the scar that spans her stomach, or the lacerations on her throat from where crackling bile poured. Girl clutches the monster eyes and reminds herself of how she got them.

Soft and Hard

ALMA KASTAN

A Letter to My Past Self

CECELIA ROSS

Dear Cece,

Today is the day you will officially decide that you have had enough of the way you look. You will become even more aware of your belly that you believe is overly large, your puffy cheeks that make you think you look like a toad, and your thighs that jiggle every time you hit a bump while riding in the car. You will finally decide to lose weight.

By causing much of your body to dissipate, you will cause your mind to become sicker and your body to start failing, and you will frustrate yourself and your family. Your disorder will make you pursue the impossibility that society imposes as the norm, allowing fat stigma and an industry that destroys innocent people to win. You will see that others who don't fit this mold are beautiful, but when you see yourself, you will let the criticism thrown toward normal-looking people seep into your self-perception.

At the moment, you are glad that the fall semester is over. You are so relieved that your family will have a chance to relax after a stressful few months of drowning in work. But you fail to recognize that you are about to put them through an equal amount of stress in the semester to come.

When you see how much pain and worry you are inflicting on your family, your intense self-hatred, regarding your mind and not just your body, will intensify. You will quickly realize that you are hurting those around you, and you will feel profoundly guilty. But by then, your anorexia will have fully developed, and you will be unable to go back. You will continue to refuse to feed yourself, and continue to wear down your patient, loving family.

In April, you will reach your weight goal. You will believe that this entirely unnecessary loss is still not enough, and continue starving yourself, always dissatisfied by how your body looks. In April, you will go to the doctor and find that you are losing not just fat, but also your bones, your muscles, your heart, and, most disturbingly, your brain. Attempting to reach societal standards of beauty will nearly end up destroying you and your body.

When you are restricting, you won't enjoy yourself. You will find yourself unable to eat anything with added sugar, and it will be hard to eat foods that don't show calorie counts. It will be awkward to hang out with friends, even if you refuse to admit it. And, because of what starvation is doing to your body, you will experience cold and achiness that you never imagined, making you shiver in pain as if you're constantly being drenched in ice water.

You will waste so much time during this semester thinking about food and weight. You will spend hours every day dreaming of cooking and eating, and even more time calculating nutrition facts. You will think about foods that you never liked and have no desire to actually eat, and they will seem unbelievably enticing. There will hardly be a moment when you can make your starving mind focus on anything other than food.

When you first go to the doctor, you won't believe you have anorexia. It will be impossible for you to understand how sick you are, and you will feel betrayed by the diagnosis. You will feel like an imposter. And you will experience intense fear and sadness that make you sob in the exam room.

During recovery, you will quickly get tired of eating amounts that make you uncomfortable, both physically and emotionally. You will feel disgusted, and highly embarrassed to be seen eating. After a while the embarrassment will fade, as well as the physical discomfort, but you will still be tired of food, and the disorder lingering in your mind will make you uncomfortable with the notion that you are trying to gain weight.

Eventually, your mind will start to become stronger than the disorder. You will have moments of confidence, and there will even be a day when, for the first time in almost a year, you voluntarily drink a milkshake. But other times, anorexia will still grip you, drowning your mind and controlling you until you try again to destroy yourself. These moments will leave you feeling so small, so ashamed.

Please understand: you are *healthy*, and you are beautiful in your own way. Please understand: real beauty comes in billions of forms and is found most of all in what makes each of us unique. In the future, I hope you will use the tools you develop during the process of recovery to help you stay stronger than the negative thoughts you have about yourself, physically *and* mentally. And I hope you will realize that there is so much to be said for looking like yourself.

Sincerely,
Cece from the Future

Me, Myself, and I

NOA KALFUS

Fairy Poem

ALIZA ABUSCH-MAGDER

Today I am visited by elementary school fairies. They tug at the sloppy braid they laced through my thinning hair. With wide eyes and the guilt-trip-inducing tone that sounds somewhat like a whine, they urge me to put down the phone. These fairies are as persuasive as the Sirens, singing, "Come play, come play." So we play.

I am absorbed into a world of fantastical indulgence. Make-believe coats reality: from the dusty corners of Abba's closet, where suits drape like dresses on our fragile bodies, to the shore, where we collect saltwater that sloshes down the sides of our Dollar Tree plastic bucket, returning to sun-crisped towels to take orders for pizza made of wet, gloppy sand. When reality interrupts our pizza party or hallway runway show, we munch on veggies cut into little sticks, we run to the bathroom and wash with lots of soap between every finger, we go to bed with the suit jacket strewn on a sandy carpet. The day is tired, and so are our soft fairy bones.

When I wake up, I am a weird brand of human: grown, scared, still tired, and eternally with a hint of dread. I seem to be rotting into one of those "adults," in the liminal space between fairyhood and adulthood—the purgatory between cotton-candy dreams and deadlines, lists, a harsh, concrete future. I tell myself, "You will always carry a bit of a fairy," because it's the truth and what I need to hear.

I am a healthy collection of hardships and blessings. I am an enjoyable amount of crazy. I have porcelain skin but am not so fragile. I have my mom's thighs and my dad's love of reading obscure Wikipedia pages. Carrot juice is my favorite color. I feed my flowers vodka and my goldfish tea biscuits. My journal thinks I am spastic and neurotic but loves me regardless, or even because. My spirit smells of fresh-out-the-oven lemon meringue. If you plant seeds in my hair, wildflowers will grow. Ice cream is my favorite food, and my favorite flavor is tired tears.

I grow and my limbs become heavy, but I am always and forever a fairy.

Sparks

FRANKIE VEGA

The other day someone asked
me about you.

I said something about your teeth and how your
smile lights up the room and about how every
freckle on your cheeks is perfectly
placed and about the way you walk as if you know
where you are going and how your knowing hands
have been callused but are still so welcoming
and how your warm brown eyes catch the sunlight
and how your curly hair flows when you're walking and
how your lips curl lovingly around your teeth
and about that one day you parted your hair in
the middle and about the way you speak like
honey is flowing out of your soul and about your
artistic mind that produces masterpieces.

And I couldn't help but notice
the familiar warmth that
your name sparks within.

Free Woman

MOLLY VOIT

CHAPTER FOUR

Traditions, Interpretations, and Imperfections

I no longer need validation from others to accept who I am.

FROM "WHY MY HAIR FALLS THE WAY IT DOES," BY MAKEDA ZABOT-HALL

*I*n our search for independence, we draw from those around us, wrestling with what to protect and what to protest. This is true as we lay claim to all of our identities, and our Judaism is no exception.

For some of us, being Jewish means lighting candles every Friday or wrapping ourselves in tefillin as we challenge gendered expectations. For others, it means grounding ourselves once a year in hushed Yom Kippur prayer, enjoying a particular sense of humor, or craving bagels and lox or freshly baked pita.

For many of us, Judaism is characterized by joy, food, and celebration. Yet histories of discrimination—both at the hands of others and among Jews ourselves—also influence our Jewish experience.

Judaism is a soft labor of love for some, a hard struggle for others. It can be the central thesis of our lives, only a footnote, or something in between.

We are guided by our ancestors while we make ritual our own in **21st-Century Amidah**.

In **My Jewish-Themed Bat Mitzvah**, the writer surprises herself by embracing tradition.

Pomegranates, bagels, and latkes: **The Art of Jewish Food**.

My Version of Practicing Judaism explores how one person integrates her physical and spiritual needs.

The speaker of **Because I Can** rises above the whispers to reclaim prayer.

Spirituality blooms in unexpected ways in **I Am Not Religious, Am I?**

Jazz is an homage to the holiness of the creative process.

A writer asks herself: am I an **Asian Jew or Jewish Asian?**

Gender identity and religious ritual part ways, then find each other again, in **L'hitateif V'l'hani'ach (To Don and To Wrap)**.

In **Why My Hair Falls the Way It Does**, the writer learns to accept who she is.

Eva captures a Holocaust survivor's pain and resilience, and the power of art to preserve our history.

My Journey to Jewishness: on being the only Jewish teen in town.

The Last Death of Jerusalem evokes the stabilizing force of faith in times of tragedy.

21st-Century Amidah

JAMIE KLINGER

Blessed are You, our God,
and God of our fathers and mothers,
who guides my fingers to strike the match
as I attempt to light the *shamash*
for the first time, as I fumble with
words that were delivered to me, born in
the Holy Land but sent through the grey
New York harbor, illuminated by false promises
paved with gold, to live hidden
in the back of my throat.

God of Abraham, God of Isaac,
and God of Jacob, the God who spins me
round and round in the most powerful
hora I've ever been in, thousands
of years, right here, grasping me in
strong arms while we dance at my
bat mitzvah.

God of Sarah,
God of Rebekah, God of Rachel,
and God of Leah, who pass their crowns
of ringlets to me, each curl
mapping my past and identifying
my tribe as *Yael*, she who is
strong, who is powerful, she
who will protect what is hers.
The great God, mighty
and awesome, who makes me high
from laughter as I paint faces
at the Purim carnival, apologizing when
I smudge the whiskers that adorn a
little boy's cheeks.

Who does acts of loving-kindness,
and creates everything, and remembers
the loving acts of my grandfather and
grandmother, who faithfully attend
our massive seder organized by family
tree, each branch coming together,
one trunk anchoring us all,
as we thrive in the country that
harbored us, the
children of their children.

A Ruler who helps, saves, and shields:
Blessed are You,
to my father Abraham
and to my mother Sarah,
who shelters me through the ages,
cradling me gently, palm to cheek,
so that I may stand, breathe in
my history, and say
Amen.

My Jewish-Themed Bat Mitzvah

ELENA EISENSTADT

A bat mitzvah, literally meaning "daughter of the commandment," is when a Jewish girl becomes a Jewish woman. But calling this tradition "ancient" would be a stretch. My great-great-aunt Judith Kaplan was the first woman to become a bat mitzvah in the United States. Recalling the day years later, she said, "No thunder sounded. No lightning struck. It all passed very peacefully." I never met Judith, but she always feels like a looming presence at the communal Jewish events I attend. After all, she is one of my family's coveted claims to fame.

So you can imagine the shock and horror on my mother's face when, while daydreaming about the impending service and party back in seventh grade, I asked without thinking, "What should my theme be?"

All the other kids at my Jewish day school had celebrations filled with Hollywood-red carpets, Eagles football paraphernalia, and *Friends* carica-tures bordering the ballroom. They all had themes. It was practically law. Halachic law.

"Your theme is Judaism," my mom declared. It wasn't up for debate.

Having a Jewish-themed bat mitzvah meant a multiday event beginning with a Friday night service, then a three-hour Saturday morning Torah reading in my first pair of heels and a matching dress with appropriate coverage, which made me sweat anxiously in the overheated chapel. It meant delaying the start time of Saturday night's party until after the Sabbath ended, and only hosting meals in a certified-kosher venue. Most importantly, it meant dancing a ten-minute hora, which I had whittled down from my parents' original idea of a two-hour one that would've "meant a lot" to the whole family—Judith Kaplan included.

So while my friends had themes that supported America's capitalist culture, my theme was a monotheistic Abrahamic religion. Definitely not as cool.

At first, I was pretty upset. To a middle schooler, this seemed like the end of the world. A good theme didn't just dictate whether or not people talked about the event. It was a way of branding yourself. It revealed your middle school passions, aspirations, and obsessions. The theme existed forever on cheap Gildan sweatshirts sporting your name and bat mitzvah date. You would always be digging out those crumpled photo booth strips from the pockets of old coats. And though, in fifteen years, you might not remember the opening line of your Torah portion, you'd undoubtedly remember your theme.

My parents argued that the point of the event was not to be a spectacle. (Apparently, they didn't believe in the whole "thunder sounding, lightning striking" idea either.) Instead, it was a sign to our Jewish community that I was coming of age. That was fine, but I felt like just being Jewish was not enough of an identity. I thought that a theme would help me assert myself as someone interesting—someone who wanted to be a movie star, or actually liked football, or had strong opinions about Ross and Rachel's relationship—as someone who was more than just Jewish.

When I was thirteen, my idea of being just Jewish revolved around the passing down of tradition, even if I didn't fully appreciate it. My ancestors read Torah on Saturday mornings, and I was charged with doing the same. Five years later, I am struck by the simplicity of my parents' wish, and my dismissiveness of the endeavor.

In February 2020, I sat through another three-hour service and watched my middle sister recite prayers in her first pair of heels and matching dress with appropriate coverage. With the pandemic in full swing, only our family stood in the overheated chapel. There was no party, and there was no theme, except Judaism. Religion in its fullest form—traditions, interpretations, and imperfections.

Judaism is no middle school fad, but its thunder sounds and lightning strikes even when the party guests are gone.

The Art of Jewish Food

DALIA HELLER

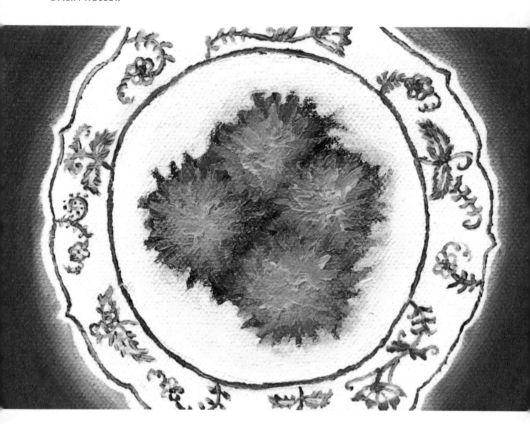

My Version of Practicing Judaism

LAUREN ALEXANDER

Throughout my life, I've done things a little differently from those around me. This is largely due to the fact I was born with a condition called cerebral palsy, or CP. CP affects my mobility, my balance, and my coordination. Because of this, I often have to make adaptations to things I do every day, including some of the ways I practice my Judaism.

For many years of my life, it was extremely difficult for me to accept doing anything in a way that was not identical to the way my peers had done it. I remember standing on the *bimah* at one of my final rehearsals for my bat mitzvah service, when I realized that there was absolutely no way for me to carry the Torah down the stairs off of the bimah, as was the traditional way of starting the processional during the Torah service. This was always at the back of my mind, but not until that moment where it was finally about to happen did I fully understand the reality of it. For one terrible moment, I stood there, paralyzed and on the verge of tears, with a despicable voice in my head telling me: *You can't do it, and that means you're a failure.* I was convinced that my inability to do something as simple as carrying a Torah scroll down a set of stairs was yet another addition to the list of things that marked me as "different," which at that time in my life seemed like the absolute worst thing in the world.

As it turned out, the solution to my problem was a relatively simple one: I started the processional directly in front of the *bimah* so I could avoid carrying the Torah down a set of stairs. While this change to my service was slight, it was still one that was completely necessary in order for it to run smoothly. And though I may not have been able to carry the Torah down a flight of stairs like everyone else had, I was able to accomplish something much bigger. Making this one tiny change to my service allowed me to leave my own very special mark on the hallowed tradition that is b'nai mitzvah.

As I've grown older, I've realized that even though I sometimes have to alter my practices in order to meet my physical needs, my spiritual connection remains entirely unaffected. My Judaism is always something that I've valued, and I will continue to do so as I begin my journey into Jewish adulthood. I also know that I will continue to practice my own unique version of Judaism, and that whatever changes I make are not something to be ashamed of.

Every Jew can have their own version of practicing Judaism. Although you may have to stray from some of the "traditional" methods, it doesn't at all mean that you're doing it wrong. In fact, the only thing that matters is practicing Judaism in whatever way you can. At the end of the day, that's going to be the only version that is right for you.

Because I Can

YAEL BEER

First you place the shel yad on the upper arm

No one dares look at her

When it's tight enough, say the blessing

Someone turns and stares

Wrap the strap around your upper arm once

Then the whispering starts

Now wrap the strap around your forearm exactly seven times

She walks toward the bimah

Put the shel rosh right between your eyes, at your hairline

Every eye is on her

Say the blessing and then say

She opens her siddur

Baruch shem k'vod malchuto l'olam va'ed

The whispering gets louder

Wrap the arm strap once around your palm

Someone says, "Isn't that unhealthy?"

Wrap the strap once around your middle finger, saying

She starts to pray

V'eirastich li l'olam

Her chin is up

Wrap it around the next knuckle, saying

Her eyes closed

V'eirastich li b'tzedek uv'mishpat uv'chesed uv'rachamim

So maybe, just maybe

Turn it back to the first knuckle

She can stop hearing their taunts

V'eirastich li be'emunah, v'yada'at et Adonai

"You're not a real Jew!"

Wrap your ring finger to your middle finger

"You don't really know anything about the Torah!"

Bring the strap back to your palm

She ignores their sneers when she reads from the Torah

Then wrap the strap around the middle of your palm, again, and again

A hand goes up to shield his eyes from the sight of a girl in tefillin

See how it looks like the word Shaddai on your hand

She leads anyway

The boxes should be right at your head

Standing tall, defying them all by learning and praying

And your heart

Inwardly deciding

This is how you wear tefillin.

I Am Not Religious, Am I?

MAYA KEREN

I'm not religious. Or at least I didn't think I was.

Raised in a secular Jewish household, I grew up associating religious holidays with comforting food and the warmth of family. Shabbat every Friday meant my dad's homemade pizza and dinner with the whole family; Passover meant my grandmother's matzah ball soup and laughing with cousins. I was never forced to go to synagogue, never made to learn Hebrew for my bat mitzvah, never discouraged from exhaling a strained "Oh my God!" in moments of exasperation. My parents, both physicians, gave me space to construct my own ideas about spirituality.

However, having two parents who studied science for the greater part of their lives leads to a certain type of childhood experience. Perhaps it was the Big Bang picture book that my mother read to me when I was five, or my father's explanation of Einstein's theory of relativity when I was ten. Maybe it was the unsettling ER stories or the occasional news of a patient diagnosed with cancer. Surrounded by the logic and reason of the physical world, I began to place my faith in science.

In my mind, there was a clear divide between science and religion. On one hand was logic—tangible, conclusive. And on the other hand was emotion—ambiguous, invisible.

Then I started playing piano.

At seven, I worked through basic classical études; now at seventeen, I play exclusively jazz. At first, practicing piano was just another box to check. Now I find that music is the closest thing I have to religion. Every day I set aside two hours of my time to play. Like a time of focused worship, each session is deliberate and demanding. Yet during these two hours, I feel a sense of release. I am deeply engaged, and at the same time, I stop thinking. Often the time stretches and slips, twisting around my fingertips—I'll look up and find it's been an hour (maybe I should tell Einstein about this trick). For me, this phenomenon is by far the most spiritual aspect of music.

And that's just solo piano. When I'm playing with other people, I feel even more that making music is quasi-religious. We communicate and bond through sound, listening much more than talking. We support each other in our different roles: the bass and drums ground the group; the piano provides the color; the horns tell the story. I meet new people through music, and we grow closer through our joint dedication to this faith.

Sometimes, listening to Miles Davis, sitting by myself as a sheet of sunlight floats through my window and illuminates the specks of dust frozen in the air, I get this itch of wonder. How does such beauty exist randomly, spontaneously, without some sort of purpose?

Music, to me, is unexplainable. Holy.

And the most mystifying thing is this: music is entirely rooted and reflected in science. We are driven to tears by simple changes in the frequencies of sound waves. We exult when certain wavelengths combine in different proportions. Just as the path of a quantum particle may take infinite forms, the journey of a jazz improvisation has infinite possibilities from the starting note to the final breath. Just as gravity establishes the foundations of what we know to be true about the physical world, the gravity of a tonal center anchors all harmony in music.

Through music, I experience spirituality, yet I also find affirmations of the fundamental laws of science. Music has helped me soften the lines of my beliefs, proving that religion can be found through the beauty of sound, in science itself.

So maybe I am religious.

Jazz

LIORA MEYER

Asian Jew or Jewish Asian?

EMMA ROSMAN

For my entire life, I've described myself using two words: Asian and Jewish. One word fits my physical identity (how the outside world perceives me), and the other fits my spiritual identity (how I see myself). The unique combination of these words shapes who I am. Lately I've been wondering which word comes first—am I an Asian Jew or a Jewish Asian?

I was adopted from China when I was fourteen months old by my parents and sister, who call themselves "classic Jews." They're short, they're white, and they have curly brown hair (except for my dad, who is super bald). I've never been bothered by the fact that my sister and I don't look alike, but I am amused by how much it confuses people. When we were little, we played a game called "How Are We Related?" with strangers. They usually thought that we were friends or distant cousins, but they never guessed that we were sisters.

People often ask me when my parents told me I was adopted. The answer is never; my parents have always made the concept of adoption familiar to me. I would have to be completely oblivious not to notice that I'm Asian and my parents are not. But my race is a much bigger factor in the way people view me than in the way I view myself.

My parents made an effort to introduce Chinese culture to me, by celebrating the Chinese New Year and taking me to festivals when I was little. They made it clear that they would always support me if I wanted to explore my culture, but I have never really been compelled to because, internally, I don't feel Chinese.

For most of my life, I didn't think deeply about being Jewish; it's just something I am. Shortly after my parents brought me home from China, I went to the mikvah and was converted to Judaism. I attended preschool at my synagogue, attended religious school from kindergarten to eighth grade, celebrated my bat mitzvah, and now work as a *madrichah*, teaching third graders how to read Hebrew. I also joined BBYO in eighth grade, which helped me to engage with my Jewish identity more than I ever had before.

My full name is Emma Yang Rosman: a weird combination of names that perfectly represents who I am. "Emma" is a tribute to my maternal great-grandfather, Eli. "Yang" is the Chinese name that I was given at the orphanage where I lived for the first year of my life. My parents chose to keep it as my middle name so I could keep a part of my Chinese identity. "Rosman" has the stereotypical Jewish "-man" ending. For a long time, I was not proud of my name. I was self-conscious about my initials because they prompted people to ask about my middle name, and I didn't tell people my middle name when they asked.

On my first day of middle school, my math teacher marked me absent by mistake. Instead of apologizing, she made the excuse that my name didn't match my face. In my first month of high school, I told my gym teacher that I would be out for a couple of days for Rosh Hashanah and Yom Kippur. He chuckled and responded with, "I guess you can never tell these days." While I don't think my teachers had bad intentions, I view these comments as pure ignorance. My teachers didn't understand that I could be both Asian and Jewish, because they had never met anyone like me or considered the fact that people like me exist. Some people do not try to understand other people's backgrounds, especially when they're not like their own. But there are things we can do to be better, such as educating ourselves about other people's cultures, and just thinking twice before we talk about things we may not know much about.

Being Asian is a part of me, but being Jewish is a bigger part. The way I am viewed by other people affects me greatly, but as cheesy as it sounds, I have always believed that it is what's inside that really counts. Despite all the ignorant comments I get from strangers, and the weird looks I get when people realize that I'm both Asian and Jewish, I am incredibly proud to call myself an Asian Jew.

L'hitateif V'l'hani'ach
(To Don and To Wrap)

ALYX BERNSTEIN

The first time I wore a tallit, I was a bar mitzvah boy. It was a traditional tallit, white with light blue stripes. It was a large tallit, but it fit perfectly. I felt proud wearing it. I was ascending to adulthood, and this was a powerful symbol of my maturity and growth. I wore it during morning prayers at school every day, along with my black leather tefillin, wrapped according to my mother's Sephardic tradition.

A year and four months later, on the last day of eighth grade, I took it off. I thought I'd never wear it again. Three months later, I came out as transgender. No longer was I a Jewish boy. My tallit and tefillin sat on my shelves, gathering dust, abandoned along with my former male identity. I didn't give the two of them much thought.

I had been wrestling with my Jewish identity. I felt that I could not be queer and Jewish at the same time, and I struggled to reconcile how the Torah talks about LGBTQ people with my own identity—both my gender and my sexuality. I didn't say the prayers at school anymore or engage in Judaism at all. I gave no thought to wearing tallit and tefillin until a group of faculty and older students scheduled a forum on women wearing tallit a few months after I came out. My school—a Conservative Jewish day school—"encouraged" girls to wear tefillin, though they had done little to put that policy into action, and some of the faculty and students wished to do more. I didn't go to the forum, mostly because of schedule, but I was intrigued.

Someone asked me what I thought of the forum, even though I hadn't attended. Of course girls should be mandated to wear tallit, I said. Nowhere in the Sh'ma does it say for only men to wear tzitzit and tefillin. God tells Moses to speak to all the Children of Israel and to tell them all to wear tzitzit and tefillin, to bind them as a sign on your arm, between your eyes, and on the corners of your garment. Why shouldn't girls do it if the boys are required?

This person responded, "So why don't you wear them?"

I had no answer. I was a feminist about Jewish ritual in theory, but I didn't particularly care at the time to put this ritual into practice, since I felt disengaged from God and the commandments. Tallit and tefillin were just another two I could not follow.

A few months later, in March of 2016, I went to a Keshet LGBTQ and Ally Teen Shabbaton. In a space that was Jewish and queer, I felt, for the first time, that I could embrace both of my identities simultaneously. I had spiritual experiences there, and over time, I came to embrace religion in my life again. I joined the traditional minyan at my school and became a leader in the larger *minyanim*. Yet I still did not put on my tallit and tefillin again. They were still too masculine for me, something I had rejected for myself.

Growing up Orthodox, I never saw women wearing tallit or tefillin. It was forbidden. Even once I moved into a more progressive, Conservative community, it was still a rare sight, especially at my school, where only a few girls wore them. I became close friends with one of those girls, who participated in the traditional minyan with me. She told me about how she had changed people's minds about women wearing tallit and tefillin. She wore her tallit and tefillin proudly as a Jewish girl. I came to realize that I could be a proud, trans, Jewish girl and wear tallit and tefillin. I deserve the same access to the holy rituals that connect the Jewish people to God.

I chose to keep my tefillin because they have a special connection to my Sephardi ancestry. However, I purchased a new tallit. I chose one featuring two biblical heroines. First, Deborah, a judge who led the Jewish people to liberation. Second, Miriam the prophetess, who stood up to the oppressive Pharaoh to save the Jewish baby boys, including her own brother.

So, for the second time, I will wear a new tallit with my tefillin. I will take an ancient tradition and make it my own. My identities are not in conflict—they are each an integral part of what makes me who I am, and I am proud of all of them.

Why My Hair Falls the Way It Does

MAKEDA ZABOT-HALL

When I was eleven years old, my father sat me down on a broken, four-legged stool that had been in our apartment for years. Facing me, he began to hum the tune of a Tracy Chapman song. I studied his long dreads and the scar he had from when he was a boy in Jamaica. I prayed the song would never end.

My father's childhood was different from mine, but I guess that's why he raised me the way he did: family-oriented and confident. He made sure to bring me to the place where his life started, not only so he would not forget, but to teach me exactly where my roots come from and why my curls fall the way they do. I remember the outline of the Blue Mountains, peaceful and untouched, the sunset melting into them. Like the sugarcane water that dripped from our mouths as my siblings and I sat eating on our grandmother's steps. The Blue Mountains, the sugarcane, and the mango trees that my father used to climb as a boy are imprinted in my head, just like my father hoped they would be.

I think of this time in the mountains when I need to remember why I grew up the way I did. Between the Jewish high holiday celebrations in Portland and Chelsea, and dumpling and curry goat dinners in Brooklyn, it was easier to say I was Jamaican and Jewish than it was for me to believe it.

When I was sixteen years old, I traveled to Israel. Being in Israel broadened my outlook on Judaism, but more importantly, it shifted my self-perception. I discovered that it does not matter if others think I am Jewish or not, because my Judaism is personal to me, and it is whatever I want it to be. All of the ideas of what a Jew is "supposed" to look like and questions like "Why is your complexion darker than your mother's?" that I had experienced in the past no longer carried the same weight. This awakening imprinted in my brain as the first time I was able not just to say I was Jewish but to believe it.

Although my identity is personal to me, my family has helped me to accept who I am. I will always remember the outline of the Blue Mountains in the town where my father grew up in Jamaica. I will remember the old siddur books in my grandfather's shul that were held by generations before me. I will remember the taste of the sugarcane water melting on my tongue. But I will also remember the harder times. What I learned was that the bad cleared the way for the good, and it gave my family room to grow and reflect, a chance to move on. I know my family isn't perfect, but neither is the process of accepting who I am.

I remember the smell of the cream that would strip my curls, making it easier for me to fit in at my Jewish day school. But that was then. Now I walk the halls of my high school with my curls coiled and bold. I wear a necklace that declares my Hebrew name, "Leah."

Now, at the age of seventeen, it has become easier to let these two parts of my identity—Jamaican and Jewish—become one. I no longer need validation from others to accept who I am. All of these memories from my childhood, good and bad, have shaped my understanding of who I am and why my hair falls the way it does.

Eva

WHITNEY COHEN

My Journey to Jewishness

EMILY DUCKWORTH

As I closed the cover of the book, I felt the world shift around me. I realized I would never view myself in the same way. At age ten I had just finished reading *Anne Frank: The Diary of a Young Girl.*

I grew up in a small, economically depressed town in rural North Carolina. My mother and I were the only Jewish people in town, there were no synagogues, and most of my peers had never met another Jewish person before. But after reading Anne Frank's harrowing story, I began to make a connection with my Jewish heritage. As I looked around my school and community, I realized that I did not quite fit in with the prevailing social milieu. Unlike all of my friends, my parents and I did not attend church on Sundays or participate in the social activities associated with church membership. I felt disconnected, like a sort of Other.

Although I did not grow up actively practicing Judaism, I recognized that being Jewish alters my relationship with the world, impacting the way others see me and the way I see myself. In subsequent years, I realized that many of my classmates were not educated about Judaism, did not respect my being Jewish, and even made anti-Semitic statements.

It was a sunny afternoon in seventh-grade science class, and before class began, my friend Kylie approached me with a Christian Bible. She shoved the book into my arms. "Here, take this. You could use it."

I stared at her. "Um, thanks, but I don't need this."

"Yes you do. So you can be saved! If you have any questions about it, I wrote down my phone number and my church's number in the back." She gave me a warm smile and headed back to her seat.

I looked at the three other students sitting at my table, silently asking if what just transpired was normal. They simply smiled at me and began taking out last night's homework.

When I was in eighth grade, it became popular to insult people by calling them "Jew." I remember being confused and outraged when I heard this. When we were studying the Holocaust, some kids made inappropriate jokes such as, "What's the difference between coal and a thousand Jews? Jews burn longer."

The prejudice I experienced over the years in my town and even within my circle of friends was eye-opening. I am grateful that I experienced a self-awakening through Anne Frank's diary. Her story drove me to learn more about my Jewish heritage and is the primary reason for my interest in politics, history, ethics, and social justice. Prior to reading the diary, I had no real grasp of humanity's capacity for hatred; nor did I understand the ability of individuals to have an impact by showing courage and mercy. Anne's story triggered my incipient understanding of righteousness and the role of human agency in the world. My experience growing up as a member of a minority group has taught me to be sensitive to other people's perspectives and needs.

Being Jewish is just one aspect of my identity, but learning more about that part has helped me to become a better person. I am more interested in the world around me and the well-being of others. Anne Frank's wisdom and tenacity continue to inspire me on my personal journey. Regardless of her circumstances, she never lost faith in the benevolence of humanity: "In spite of everything, I still believe people are good at heart."

The Last Death of Jerusalem

AYDIA CAPLAN

The woman with no name laid her hand on the soft, crumbling stone. She spidered her fingers along the uneven lines between bricks and twined them into moss embroidered black by the night.

Something fell from a crack in the wall, and she looked at it, feeling that she, too, was being watched from above. Then, because there was nothing else to do, she sighed and picked it up: paper someone long ago had pressed into niches between stones. She unfolded it. Took in the gliding shapes of words.

By now her body had learned to carry on—to reach for the things in front of it. Her fingers crept into a different crack in the wall, extracted a different wad of paper. She couldn't read this language either, but she knew it: detached letters, vowels sucked out, the language of prayer. Yes, this was a small slip of faith; they all were.

She recognized this wall. She'd known of it long before the day she woke up one morning, lost and alone in this foreign land.

A shadow crossed her face as she stepped back and gazed around her. So she was in Jerusalem.

Why?

A once-theoretical God had chosen her, of all the people in the world, to be condemned to this isolation. This question had been her life since she woke up alone: an endless *Why me?*, sometimes *Why am I hated by a God I don't even know?* But now: *Why Jerusalem?*

She leaned against the wall and looked out over the plaza. Jerusalem, a ghost town in a ghost world. The misery of this once-holy land echoed in her heart, numbing her inside and out. Collapsed buildings, fractured tiles. The wind, carrying the scent of dust and ash, sighed as it rushed through hollow spaces. The tightly folded prayers in the Western Wall whispered.

All around her were the dead. She could almost feel them, scores of them, not risen even though the world had ended. It hadn't been a surprise that all the people were gone. Everyone had known it was coming. They had prepared to die; she had prepared.

The unbelievable part was that she was still here.

Leaning against the Western Wall, she stood alone in the derelict holiness, the resting place of kings upon kings.

She turned back to the wall. Her eyes measured out the distance above her: heart-thuddingly high. But she had nothing to lose, nothing at all. And perhaps this was what the wrathful God wanted: the last human to end herself in fear and faith, now that this terrible miracle had made her a believer.

She found crevices in the wall for her hands, held it like a dance partner. Clumps of paper loosened and pattered below her as she placed her toes carefully on the cold stone, pulled upward, brought knee to ribs searching for another foothold, pushed down with her right hand to reach up with her left. At last she heaved herself onto the top and stood there, hair billowing. Surrounding her was open space and God and Jerusalem.

The feeling of being watched was chased away by a great, hounding numbness. Twilight rustled around her in the wind, cloaking the remains of buildings, beckoning her to the edge where she stood gazing at the city. Her gaze roved over the tumbled houses and streets, over the broken dome like an egg hatched empty. The city that had weathered so many attacks finally lay obliterated, and impious she was the only one to see it.

No—what did it matter that she was in Jerusalem? The whole world was hell, so what did it matter? She was beyond isolation: there was nothing left to isolate herself from. Language had no words to describe this solitude, but there was no need for language now, no need for names. So why her, nameless and wandering? And why the paper, why the wall, why the city?

She almost jumped then, out of sheer fury. Just to defy a God that had been nowhere and now was everywhere, who had chosen her to live on and transplanted her into a city that was everything beautiful and gone. Just to see if God would let her fall.

She stepped to the edge. She rocked on her toes, back and forth, now hovering over the expanse of darkness, now standing solid on rough-hewn rock.

Why did she hesitate? She had been ready for this. She hadn't been one of those who had raged against the end and gone screaming and thrashing into the fire. She had been ready to close her eyes and let it wash over her. She was ready still.

She leaned forward. Death was just in front of her, just one step out, and there was God, and they had been so distant but now they were close enough to touch. Her eyes closed.

She exhaled.

And she felt it, crashing through her like fire, glowing within. Her breath. She was alive. She was alive, she was alive.

She opened her eyes and saw the stars that were so far away from each other but blazed anyway, blazing out a wild breadth of beauty. Below, some of the trees were still reaching upward—they had survived the second flood, the flood of fire that she never saw. She was Noah. The city was wrecked but magnificent, and she had been chosen to see it.

She filled her lungs with Jerusalem and felt sacred. God had taken her here and given her life, and everyone was gone but she was still here.

On the wall of a thrice-demolished temple, she threw her head back and screamed, one long pure note, a grief cry, the only sound, which echoed into the night and touched every part of the city and settled into the rubble to stay there forever.

She inhaled again. She climbed down the Western Wall and stared at that vertical garden of wishes. At last she picked up a stone and scraped words directly onto the wall, her first and last prayer: *Give me the strength to live.*

And the nameless woman turned and walked away from Jerusalem.

CHAPTER FIVE

Where Is the Peace?

If normalcy exists, I want it to be a normal where people don't have to hide who they are.

FROM "WHAT FREEDOM MEANS TO ME," BY LIEL HUPPERT

The Torah teaches us to recognize that we are all equally sacred. And yet, our daily lives can send us a different message. We are degraded as we dress, speak, learn, and pray. We feel injustice in our bones, our minds, our hearts.

Because of the unique identities we hold, however, oppressive forces weigh on each of us differently. Although we are all young Jews, some of us are challenged because of whom we love, how we move through the world, how we are perceived. So our experiences of injustice and our complicity vary immensely. While some of us are victims of patriarchy and white supremacy, and while many of us take actions that uphold them, we also work to dismantle these harmful systems.

We strive to unlearn and relearn. We stand up to those who cause us harm, have tough conversations with loved ones, and try to be true to ourselves. We take up our pencils, paints, and cameras to tell our personal stories, and hope they will resonate.

After a shopkeeper hurls a racist slur at the writer's father, she demands, **Where Was the "Peace" Four Hundred Years Ago?**

Facing injustice alone can fling us toward **Wit's End**.

Glancing over her shoulder at night, the speaker is certain that **You Have Not Walked the Same Streets As Me**.

Aching in high heels and holding up protest signs, **I Am a Feminist**.

What Freedom Means to Me calls on us to approach one another with empathy.

When My Friend Was Sexually Assaulted shows how vital it is to believe a survivor—especially when others don't.

Power can look many ways, as in **Feminine Strong**.

In **What You See**, the writer stands up against the insidious anti-Semitism that corrupts her Holocaust class.

Kotel of My Dreams depicts one artist's vision of a harmonious Jewish future.

Kyke Dyke opens up space for queer Jews to move from the margins to the mainstream.

A writer sends **A Message from a Jew with a Touch of Color** to those who do not see her for who she is.

Until Supreme Court Do Us Part reminds us that the personal and political are intertwined.

In **The Love You Carry**, grandparents embrace a grandchild coming out.

Where Was the "Peace" Four Hundred Years Ago?

MAKEDA ZABOT-HALL

My father is the most peaceful man I know.

A few years ago, he came home from the watch store and told us that the owner had said to him, "What would people think if they walked in and saw a nigger working here?" after my father had casually said something about becoming his apprentice and learning how to fix watches. In that very moment, I wish my dad hadn't been the peaceful man that he is.

"...a nigger working here..."

I think about this story frequently. I was so angry at my father for not screaming in the owner's face or arguing with him until he had lost his voice. My father had let me down. I wanted him to fight, but I never told him this.

A few weeks ago, in an argument, I brought this story up again, and in an instant I finally revealed to my father how I truly felt. How I felt about him walking out the door before an argument could even begin. How his actions made me lose faith in his ability to defend the color of my skin. As he listened to my concerns, with his legs crossed and his eyes calm but focused, he soaked up the emotion that poured out of his eighteen-year-old daughter. That day, my father told me that if he had gotten into an argument, he would have been risking his daughters having a future without a father or his sons having to lock the door at night, because they would now be the oldest men in the house. He wanted to fight, but he had to choose.

I thought my father hadn't fought that day because he gave in. I thought he had let them win, when in reality, he had decided that his life, vows, and the promises that he had made to his wife and children trumped everything. His family was more important than defending the color of his skin in that rundown watch shop. My father decided to swallow his anger in the face of a man who only saw his Black skin, a man who perceived my father's brown eyes as more threatening than the small pocketknife dangling from his own jeans.

My father chose us. He chose to come home instead of lying on a rug in a pool of blood, alone, and unable to defend the skin that would be soaked in the very red that is printed on the flag of a country that promised to protect him.

There will be more racist shop owners, there will be more blood, there will be more sons and daughters waiting on the stoop for their fathers who are never coming home.

Who's gonna raise the kids of the parents who were murdered screaming "George Floyd"? Who's gonna carry the body of a young Black man who has not even graduated high school yet?

My father is the most peaceful man I know, and I love him for that. But I won't wait for my brothers to be the next young Black men that "fit the description." I want to see my thirteen-year-old brother graduate from middle school.

I want to be peaceful, but where was the peace when my people hung from trees, naked and stripped of their lives? Where was the peace when Emmett Till was mutilated and murdered at the age of fourteen?

Where was the peace when unarmed Breonna Taylor was shot eight times in the comfort of her own home? Where was the peace when two men in a pickup truck chased Ahmaud Arbery, an innocent man, and fired a shotgun into his stomach?

We need more peaceful people like my father, but I won't wait for his blood to be spilled.

So let me ask you again,

Where was the peace four hundred years ago?

Wit's End

ANNIE POOLE

You Have Not Walked the Same Streets As Me

LILY PAZNER

You have not walked
The same streets as me

You have not walked the streets
Worrying about how fast
You can get to your car
Because a stranger is following you on his bike
Trying to make small talk
About how "nice" you seem

You have not walked the streets
Wondering why the older drunk man
Stopped flirting with the waitress outside the bar
to turn his attention to you and your friends
Who are only thirteen years old

You have not walked the streets
Making sure that your shorts aren't too short
Or your top too revealing because
These men do not understand
That your clothes are not consent
That your clothes do not
Give them permission to violate your body
Or to verbally assault you

You have not walked the streets
Worrying about what is ahead or who is watching
And the all-consuming fear
That makes you long for
The ignorance of your sheltered youth
Taken too soon by
Prying eyes unwanted remarks
And hands that do not know the definition of consent

You have not walked
The same streets as me
And I hope you never will

I Am a Feminist

EMILY KNOPF

I am a Feminist
I wake up with a messy bun
And stare at my reflection in
The mirror with disgust
I am a Feminist

I imprison my chest in a cage of cotton and wire
It digs into my skin
A cotton strap droops off my shoulder
I put it away because it is
Unseemly
Hanging below my sleeve line
I am a Feminist

I put a blade to my smooth hair and watch as it leaves
Bloody scars in its path
I bask in the baby-like quality of my skin
And grin
I am a Feminist

I color my face in with harshly bright
Harshly heavy
Powder
And draw and erase
Draw and erase
Draw and erase
Until my white canvas is left red
And then I cover it with white again
Because it's fun
I am a Feminist

I slide my hem along my thigh
Until it hits a place that's not too high
Or low
So that my knees still show
But not too much
Because I don't want to give the
Wrong Idea
I am a Feminist

I look both ways
As I sneak a brightly wrapped secret
Into my sleeve
And I heave
As it tumbles from my grasp
I pick it up before anyone sees
The atrocity
With rosy cheeks I scramble away
I am a Feminist

When the hairdresser asks how much to
Cut off
I hesitate
But then say "just a trim"
I am a Feminist

He bumps into me and I apologize
He talks over me and I apologize
He says he's right and I say "I know"
I am a Feminist

I hold up signs for a right to choose
As my ankles ache
In high heel shoes
And am proud that
I can exercise my own
Right

I am a Feminist

What Freedom Means to Me

LIEL HUPPERT

Because I am a special needs person, I'm not always accepted wherever I go. I have autism, ADHD, anxiety, social anxiety, depression, and bipolar II disorder. In my old school, no one really had patience for me. I got bullied for things I couldn't control. For example, I used to rock back and forth so much that people looked at me weirdly. I had a lot of different behaviors that people didn't see as "normal." But I'm a huge believer that there is no such thing as "normal."

When I was younger, I didn't always understand things that people normally would, so I asked a lot of questions. "Why?" was always my go-to question. Because people didn't know how to answer me, I often didn't get answers at all. I needed the word *no* explained to me, because I didn't understand why I couldn't do or have certain things. My uncle is a great example. We didn't have the best relationship due to the "no" problem. But we came to an understanding once he started explaining why he said no. Soon it wasn't necessary for him to go over it because I was finally understanding why people had to say no. Sometimes it was for my safety, something they couldn't provide at the time, money, and many other reasons I soon became able to figure out or guess on my own. It took someone understanding me for me to finally understand others.

I don't know why it's so hard for people to accept others and understand that not all people are the same. I used to think my special needs were a setback, but oh, was I wrong. It may have taken me a little bit longer than others to grow up, but now I understand things in a way that I never thought I could. I think so outside the box that there is no box. I can decipher metaphors, and I can understand people's behavior to the point where I have patience for almost anyone. I was never the best with social cues, and they are still hard, but I am learning to understand them better and still working on them to this day. Although I'm not the most outgoing person, I feel I have opened the eyes of those who are close to me. Knowing that I can help people understand about people like me, even if it's only a few people, makes me feel there is hope. Not everyone thinks their voice can be heard. I hope I can change that with the people who hear my story.

It breaks my heart to see people bullying others just because they talk weirdly or walk funny or look funny. When I was bullied, I felt like I was in shackles. I had to deal with all the hurtful words every day like I was in a dodgeball game, and every ball that hit me was a hurtful message, and I couldn't do anything about it. No one really ever believed me when I told them someone was saying these things to me or this is what I was going through. I felt like my hands were tied behind my back. We shouldn't have to be embarrassed because of who we are; we should embrace it!

I know I said I didn't believe in the word "normal." However, if normalcy exists, I want it to be a normal where people don't have to hide who they are. I want to see a normal where you don't even have to think twice or do a double take when someone in a wheelchair rolls by, or when someone who seems to be in their own world is enjoying just being free, walking around and doing what they do.

Our world needs more love in it; we all have to feel it. I believe that it's there waiting to be seen and heard. We just need to be the ones who listen. We just need to be the ones who open up our hearts and minds.

When My Friend Was Sexually Assaulted

ABIGAIL WINOGRAD

She sat down with the boy's parents over ceramic cups of coffee
And held her hands together like two swords before battle
And I was so proud of her
But the boy's parents swatted his wrist and winked
Grinning as silver dollars leapt from their tongues
Laughing, "Can we push this under the rug?"
And I was still so proud of her

Feminine Strong

RACHEL KAUFMAN

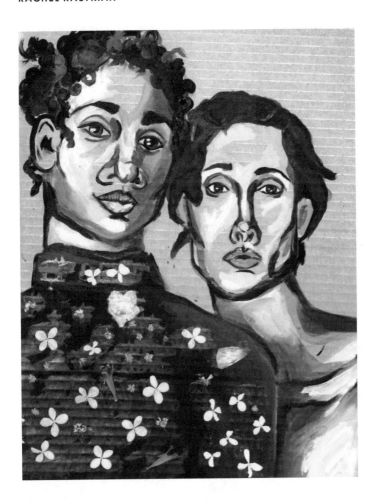

What You See

SAMARA HAYNES

You think that the class "Holocaust, Genocide, and Modern Humanity" is kind of a downer. I walk in, the only sophomore and Jew in a room full of uninterested seniors, and sit next to you after I recognize you from Instagram.

You're taking this class as a way to get an easy A, and because you heard the teacher doesn't assign much homework. I'm taking this class because it teaches the history of the greatest tragedy my family has endured, and because the teacher's son is in Hebrew school with my little sister.

When you see pictures of emaciated women in striped uniforms, you are surprised; it makes you uncomfortable. These images are not new to me; I feel no shock. I search for recognition in each face, knowing that I could find myself staring at my own reflection through the screen.

You glance at me when the teacher talks about descendants of survivors and fidget with a pen on your desk. I stand proud and share the story of my great-grandfather, whose name I will carry to future generations.

You look at your phone as the speaker's presentation reaches its thirtieth minute, bored of this field trip only one hour in. I hold back tears while a man I have never met shares the story of losing his whole family in a single day.

You stare at me as our tour guide leads us through the Holocaust Museum exhibit and whisper to your friend, "She kind of looks like Anne Frank." My face turns red; I move to the other side of the group.

Someone draws a swastika on the table in the cafeteria. You roll your eyes and say, "It's just a drawing. Why do we have to talk about this anyway?" I know that this symbol is only the start.

You post on Instagram, "If people could hide from Nazis in attics for months, we can survive a few weeks of quarantining at home." I type a comment and then delete it, worried that even after a semester-long course on the subject you choose not to see the disrespect and ignorance you are displaying.

I leave this class with college credit and infinite pride in my heritage. I hope you leave knowing why my synagogue has security guards outside.

Kotel of My Dreams

DINA OCKEN

Kyke Dyke

SARAH YOUNG

Kyke dyke.
That's what they used to call me.
So funny,
Watch me laugh.
I see the appeal.
It's short,
It's catchy,
It rhymes.
But I'm a poet now,
And I know that things don't have to rhyme,
And that sometimes when they do,
They're tacky.
Or forced.
I used to hear snickers
As I walked down the halls.
People would whisper
"Kyke dyke"
Like I couldn't hear them,
Like it wouldn't matter if I did.
And then I looked to the Jewish community,
And I found Keshet.
I found other queer Jews,
Like the fearless queer hipsters at KlezKanada.
I even met other kyke dykes:
Yona,
Who I worked with on the newspaper,
And who always knows just what to say.
Alyx,
Whose voice is always raised
For those who cannot defend themselves.
Rachel,
An incredible friend
And wonderful person.
I saw the beauty
In being a Jewish lesbian,
In finding love
With a strong Jewish woman,

The product of thousands of years
Of oppression and resurgence.
I saw the beauty
In knowing that God wants us to be happy
With each other.
Kyke dyke became a battle cry,
Something I call myself.
Something my friends and I are proud to call each other.
We were created by God as we are:
Holy kyke dykes.

A Message from a Jew with a Touch of Color

NAOMI KITCHEN

I am Syrian, Hawaiian, Colombian, Korean, Israeli, Persian, Mexican, Native American, Scottish, Cambodian, and Indian...or at least that's what some people think. In fact, I come from an Israeli American mother with a head of big, black curls and glowing olive skin, which I've inherited from her. My *saba* and *savta*, my mother's parents, are proud Israelis, children of Holocaust survivors. My *savta* loves to tell me about the time growing up in Israel when her Ashkenazi friend's mother yelled at her in Polish to stop playing with the "dirty Sephardic" (my *savta*). I have also been inundated with stories of my mother being called "*shvartza*," the Yiddish slur for "Black," by the other Jewish kids in her own childhood.

I come from a half-white, half-Korean father, from whom I've inherited every facial feature. His father comes from a family living in America since the time of the Mayflower. His mother, who raised him, is a Korean immigrant. To this day, my Korean grandmother calls herself "Oriental," and her favorite feature of mine is my big (un-Asian) eyes.

I have lived in Pittsburgh for ten years, since I was seven. I studied at the community day school through eighth grade. I've tried all the Jewish youth groups; prayed at Reform, Conservative, and Orthodox synagogues; attended Jewish summer camps; celebrated my bat mitzvah; learned to speak, read, and write Hebrew; studied abroad with a high school program in Israel for two months; joined with family and friends for Shabbat dinner almost every Friday night of my life; participated in IAC and AIPAC conferences; worked as an editor for a Jewish magazine; entered the JCC at least three times a week; and I have decided to enlist in the IDF next year. You get it—I'm Jewish, right? Yeah, you'd think.

Despite these experiences, my Jewishness is often up for debate. Why is that? I can tell you in one word: color.

I don't have a lot of "color." Sometimes I am immediately recognized as a "person of color," while other times, I'm assumed to be a white Jew.

In my ninth-grade math class, I was put in a study group with two other students. One of them asked me the classic question: "What are you?"

Before I could answer, he started guessing ethnicities. The other boy in my group, who had previously seen me in Jewish spaces, said, "Are you stupid? She's just white and Jewish." Boy number one responded by asking if boy number two was stupid. This back-and-forth continued for a while. I had always known that some people saw my "color" the moment they laid eyes on me, whereas others had to see proof of my one Korean grandmother to believe it. But this was the first time I wondered if, when I have been accepted without question as a Jew, my color was invisible. To Jews, did my color either cancel my Jewishness or my Jewishness cancel my color, never coexisting? I can't explain why some people see me as a person of color and why others do not, but what I have settled on is that, at the least, I am not completely white. I have a touch of color.

My touch of color is why I've received undeserved (but appreciated) welcomes in Native American flea markets out West and other spaces with people of color. It is also why I've received coldness and funny looks in some Jewish spaces. Racism in America's Jewish community is pervasive.

But, in my experience, Pittsburgh's Jewish community is one of the most welcoming American Jewish communities. My Jewish day school is an actively anti-racist environment. My teachers are visionary educators who have cultivated an environment of acceptance by leading conversations about *tikun olam*, racism, and injustice at every opportunity. All Jewish institutions should follow their lead.

In my community, overt racism is not the problem. The problem is the assumption that all Jews are white—fully white. They are not. We are not. This assumption must be challenged and rooted out, for if we allow it to persist we will lose our Jews of color. The coldness that I have felt in too many Jewish spaces pushes me into the arms of groups that have no real claim to me, but look at me as if they do, as if I am theirs. Because of this absurdity, I must constantly remind myself who I am. I am Jewish.

I love Pittsburgh's Jewish community with all my heart. This is why I fervently want us to be better. I ask this for myself and for other Jewish children of color: when you see us in Jewish spaces, do not give us confused, cold looks. Look at us like we are yours, because we are.

Until Supreme Court Do Us Part

GERTIE ANGEL

The Love You Carry

SYDNEY SCHULMAN

When I realized that I was bisexual, I was over the moon with excitement. All at once, parts of myself that had formerly confused me began to make sense. I saw myself and my surroundings in a new, clearer light. Finally, I understood how I could feel love in a way that would allow me to fully and properly give love.

But there was a second feeling almost directly after my euphoria. A feeling of unease and fear, despite all the positives that came with this self-discovery. Though I was looking forward to being honest with friends and family, I was also afraid.

I was frustrated that I'd have to endure this fear repeatedly. After coming out to my parents, I'd have to do it again. And again. And again. That's something people don't often tell you about coming out—you're constantly doing it. Yes, there was that important moment with my mother when the shock on her face carved a pit in my stomach, though it was followed by a promise that she supported me. When I came out to my best friend, my heartbeat was so prominent that it seemed audible—my heart exposing itself for the occasion. Yes, there are deep conversations with the people closest to you. But there are also more casual ways to admit your identity. For example, last week, an acquaintance at work asked me if I had a boyfriend at school. To this, I replied with little hesitation, "No. But I have a girlfriend. She's the coolest."

Since discovering that I was bisexual, I've come out countless times, and I know I will countless more. Still, I believe that, for everyone, there's always that one person (or set of people) to whom coming out seems the most monumental. For me, these people were my grandparents. Coming out to them was equal parts scary and crucial. I felt I had to do it, but I was scared of the capacity it had to change everything.

As their firstborn grandchild, I have always had a unique bond with my grandparents. They show great passion and interest in being a part of my life, and for that I am forever grateful. They spoil me. Not with material items, but with sincere devotion to helping me learn and grow. My grandparents are my wisest teachers and most loyal friends. They also make me sound cooler than I actually am to all of their golf buddies. Because of the irreplaceable role they play in my life, I thought it was only fair that they knew about every part of it.

So, I took them out to dinner and planned to tell them the truth. At first, I was nervous to alter my relationship with them in any way. They practice more Conservative Judaism (in comparison to my parents and me, who are Reform) and grew up in a different generation, one that was even further from LGBTQ+ equality than we are now. Since I was young, I've always wanted to make them proud of me.

At that dinner, even with all of my hesitations, I decided that in order for anyone else to be proud of me, I had to make myself proud. No matter the results, I needed to have pride in every aspect of my identity. Those who truly love me, I thought, should love every part of me. Not just curated pieces.

With this in mind, I told my grandparents that I was bisexual and currently dating a girl. Then I held my breath and didn't let it go until I heard my grandpa say, "Are you happy?"

I told him yes.

He said, "Then I am happy."

About three weeks after that dinner was prom. At my school, taking pictures before the dance is always a big part of the event, and my class was encouraged to have their families participate. After coming out to my grandparents and having it go well, I decided to invite them, along with my parents and siblings.

Here's another thing they don't tell you about coming out: it makes you free. Suppressing my sexuality was like carrying a backpack of rocks. Each time I came out to a new person in my life, I took one rock out of the bag. Each time, I became lighter and a little bit closer to being airily, completely, incredibly free.

On prom night, I felt weightless. I laughed with my friends, held my girlfriend's hand, and wrapped my arms around her for pictures. According to my sister, I was smiling wider than she had ever seen.

After my mom finished taking pictures of my girlfriend and me sticking out our tongues and smiling at the camera, my grandparents approached me. I grinned and hugged them, thanking them for coming. In return, they just pulled me close and told me they loved me. While he was hugging me, my grandpa whispered to me: "Of all the things I've seen in my life, the love you carry in your heart is the most impressive." When my grandma hugged me, she pulled me into her own whisper. She had to get on her tiptoes because of how tall I was in heels. She whispered: "You're constantly amazing us with your beauty and strength, young lady."

Some days are heavier than others. Some days, there are snide comments from ignorant classmates. Other days, slurs are murmured under breaths, full of cowardly hate. There have even been times where relationships with friends, family members, and teachers have been altered or ended as a result of my transition into embracing my sexuality. There are times when it feels difficult to be me, and in these times I find comfort in reminding myself how lucky I am to carry the love I do.

On prom night, there was a pretty impressive sunset. My girlfriend and I love sunsets, so we watched this one closely. We saw it start with the spilling of pink, yellow, and orange hues—and watched it conclude with a dusty glaze of deep violet. I like to watch sunsets because they reveal certain unarguable truths. They are nature's embodiment of the phrase "at the end of the day."

At the end of the day, when the sun's light drips away from the sky, love remains a constant source of illumination. We continue to love, because love was there in the beginning, and love will be there in the end.

At the end of the day, love liberates us all.

CHAPTER SIX

Carving Our Own Footsteps

We choose to transform our words into actions.

FROM "UPON THE DUST OF OUR ANCESTORS," BY MICHAL SPANJER

Our personal experiences of privilege and oppression call us to collectively transform the stratified, unjust world in which we live—not just for ourselves, but for all people. Feminism teaches us that none of us are free until all of us are free. Judaism teaches us that it is not our obligation to complete the work, yet we are not free to desist from it.

We draw strength from our ancestors, who have shouldered immense weight. While they grieved, they, too, created art. When confronted with injustice, they, too, took to the streets. We look to our past as we move toward justice, channeling our shyness, outspokenness, vulnerability, and bravery into action. We find comfort in community and power in coalition.

As we reflect on where we came from, who we are, and who we want to become, we ask ourselves: where do we go from here?

In **What Did We Talk About Before Corona?**, we eavesdrop on one person's inner monologue set against a larger political soundscape.

In **Mending the Broken**, we protest the murders of Black people and fight for racial justice.

The tentacles of the patriarchy pervade our lives in **The Man**.

Behind Bars humanizes those caught up in our racist carceral system.

Our Jewish values fuel our collective action against gun violence in **The Power of Jewish Youth**.

We memorialize the Black lives lost to state violence in **Say His Name, Say Their Names**.

Two Lefts and Then a Right on Orange Grove Boulevard bears witness to communal injustice.

We harness our power to make **Demands** as we march for gender equality.

Nameless Courage: the fire that sustains us.

Art is a form of environmental activism in **Dump and Burn**.

In **To My Grandfather: My Introduction to Climate Organizing**, we are in conversation with those who fought before us.

At last, we come full circle to stand **Upon the Dust of Our Ancestors**.

What Did We Talk About Before Corona?

MOLLY VOIT

My mom won't let me take the subway. This is crazy. I can't believe this is happening. We're living in historic times. Did you wash your hands? It's just a cold; I don't have corona. *Harvey Weinstein Sentenced to 23 Years in Prison.* I started wearing a mask on the train. I can't even. This is unreal. Ugh, Key Food is out of Häagen-Dazs. Did you watch the debates? *Major Sports Leagues in the U.S. Halt Play.* Wash your hands before you sit down. No more school? No Prom? NO GRADUATION? Fuck that. LOL, look at this meme. *Join Zoom meeting.* I can't believe my grandparents are still leaving their house. I learned how to play guitar today. Both of my grandparents have pneumonia. *President Trump Declares a National Emergency.* My mom won't let me have visitors anymore. Stop blaming China. WASH YOUR FUCKING HANDS. *Restaurants, Nightclubs, Movie Theaters Closed.* If the subways are running tomorrow, I'll bring you a brownie. I'm going for a walk. Don't touch your face. My friends are home from college, but I can't even see them. The trip I was looking forward to my whole life was canceled because of a fucking virus. *U.S. Federal Reserve Cuts Its Target Interest Rate to Zero.* I miss you. It's been three days. These are historic times. The season is suspended, not canceled; keep training. I have no motivation. *Here Are the Main Coronavirus Myths We're Seeing That You Should Watch Out For.* This is the worst possible way for high school to end. This is a good time for you to repair your relationship with your brother, you know. *This Is a War.* How am I supposed to work from home and help my kid attend online classes? I love you. I can't be stuck in here with you anymore. What did we talk about before corona?

Mending the Broken

SONJA LIPPMANN AND ZOE OPPENHEIMER

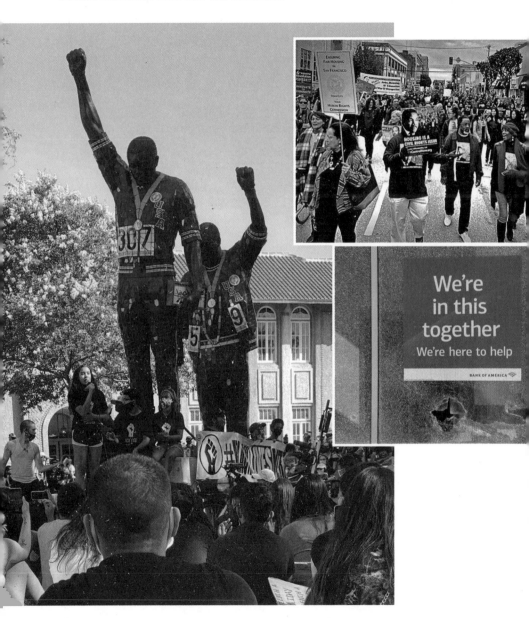

The Man

EMILIA COOPER

The man
The man who roams the earth
Breaking hearts and breaking bones
The man who flaunts his white privilege
And mistreatment of women
The man who believes
That he is deserving of more love than he gives to others
The man who doesn't see people
Only possessions
The man who treats others
Like they owe their submission to him
The man who is proud
Of his own wrongdoings
The man who has immense confidence
Because it is other people's responsibility to make him feel that way
The man who was taught growing up
That he matters more than others
The man who declares himself
The true victim of society's sexist teachings
The man who has never been told
No
The man who doesn't understand the word
No
The man who
Runs the world

Behind Bars

TALI FEEN

The Power of Jewish Youth

OFEK PREIS

On February 14, 2018, the Marjory Stoneman Douglas High School massacre became the deadliest high school shooting in US history. The gunman, who had made disturbing anti-Semitic and racist posts on social media, opened fire with a semiautomatic rifle for six minutes, killing seventeen and injuring seventeen others. This tragedy had a widespread impact and sparked discussion about school safety across the nation. Many Jewish Americans began to express concerns for their safety, for the student body at Marjory Stoneman Douglas is over 40 percent Jewish.

My high school on Long Island, New York, is closely tied to the Jewish community in Parkland, Florida, where the shooting took place. Many of my peers had become friends with MSD students through Jewish summer camps and youth social organizations, and many Parkland parents are alumni of our high school. Although I personally did not know members of the Parkland community, I commiserated with them as they expressed feelings of helplessness and being ignored. I deeply sympathized with the frustrated survivors in feeling that their call for action was not heard. *Why isn't anyone listening? Why are adults so comfortable belittling children who are crying for help?* I thought to myself. The tenacious students of Marjory Stoneman Douglas subsequently established Never Again MSD, a political action committee advocating for tighter gun regulations. To me, this epitomized self-determination and personal agency.

This initiated a period of self-reflection on my own shortcomings when it comes to advocacy. While I was often a very passionate participant in discourse about activism, my actions rarely followed suit. I realized it was time to focus my efforts on the causes that I support beyond simple conversations.

Inspired by the Parkland students who were protesting for safety and justice, I joined some of my peers in planning a school-wide walkout on the one-month anniversary of the shooting. After weeks of drafting speeches, scheduling meetings with the principal, painting banners, and garnering attention through social media, approximately 85 percent of our student body came together to memorialize the victims and advocate for school safety reform. We received extensive support from our whole community; from families of students, teachers, and staff; and even residents of Parkland.

Ten days after participating in the walkout, I traveled to Washington, DC, to attend the March for Our Lives with United Synagogue Youth, a Jewish teen movement that I had been a member of a few years prior. We met at a synagogue in Washington, DC, which hosted me and nearly one thousand other Jewish teenagers from across the US.

After we welcomed Shabbat with candle lighting and Kiddush, we talked about *tikun olam*—how we wanted to help repair our broken world. I was inspired to hear so many of my peers share their experiences with using religion to motivate advocacy. I mentioned that growing up in Israel, I had often heard the ancient proverb in Judaism: "If I don't fight for myself, who will fight for me?" I explained that Judaism often encourages personal autonomy and self-advocacy, but it is hard to stay motivated when adults often dismiss the voices of the young. Many of the other USY teenagers in the room agreed that it was inspiring to witness students our age take matters into their own hands and create a national movement.

The next morning, we marched down Pennsylvania Avenue holding signs and chanting traditional USY songs. I felt at home, surrounded by similarly minded, motivated people inspired by our shared culture. This was the first time I had ever personally witnessed how Judaism inspires solidarity in times of hardship. It illuminated the power in Jewish youth, and how Jewish identity can collectively remind us of our ethical responsibilities.

Compelled to sustain this momentum of activism, I have continued to do my part. When I attended a Black Lives Matter protest in Cedarhurst, New York, in June 2020, I reminisced about my empowering experience in Washington. There were many Jews and Israelis in attendance, and I saw many signs in Hebrew, many with motivational Torah verses. It surprised me to see so many onlookers recognize the language and decide to suddenly join and show their support for the cause. Being surrounded by supporters who share my Jewish values and are encouraged to continue their fight for social justice reminded me of the unity I felt during the march in Washington.

Since the start of the pandemic, participating in advocacy has become more difficult, which caused me to question how I will continue building on my momentum. Thanks to the internet, however, activism was not limited to the confines of our homes while we were in quarantine. In this day and age, social media is a crucial platform for engaging in conversations about activism and advocacy. The popular app TikTok has recently created a platform known as "JewTok" for Jewish millennials and Gen-Zs to make connections with fellow Jews and discuss their experiences with anti-Semitism. During the start of quarantine, I began to use my TikTok account more frequently to discuss many things I was passionate about, including advocacy. I was instantly welcomed by fellow Jews from around the globe who wanted to engage in conversation about social justice and human rights. I began to participate in discussions about anti-Semitism and racism, sharing my experiences as an Israeli immigrant in America and describing the protests I've attended. While my original goal was to refrain from participating in activism only with my words, quarantine reminded me that conversations about advocacy are an equal contributor in the fight for justice. I am so very grateful for this platform and hope to continue to use it to shed light on topics such as racial justice, intersectional feminism, anti-Semitism, and other human rights issues with my newfound community of fellow young Jews.

Say His Name, Say Their Names

GERTIE ANGEL

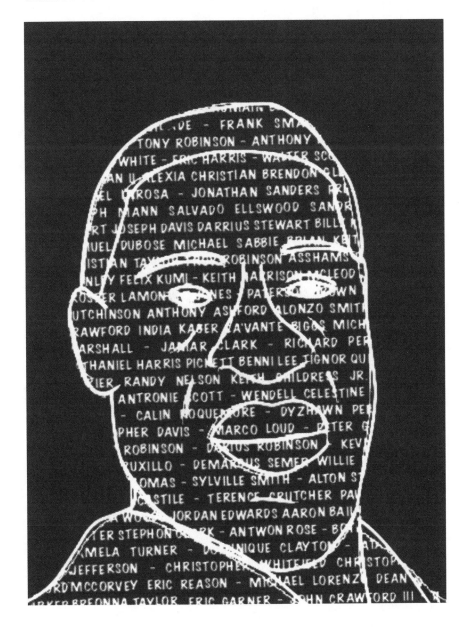

Two Lefts and Then a Right on Orange Grove Boulevard

MAYA SAVIN MILLER

I read recently
that pasadena
was the last city
in the
united states
of america
to desegregate
its school system.
And i don't know
if that metronome
beats true but
it makes sense now
why the freeway reminds me
of hand-drawn parentheses
slash
why when i ask what
is north of the one-ten
they say
we don't go there
slash
why the girl
sucking fentanyl
off the curved edge
of a blade
like a mouth torn open
at the seams
was sent to mexico
slash
why it makes sense that
people here only scream
underwater like
bars holding

a cracked window
like blinds always drawn
slash
why the constant glow
of christmas lights means
they never fixed
the lamppost
never fixed
the drunk boy
with a windshield-shaped hole
in his forehead.
We don't go there
like trying
to make us all
forget to leave
tethered
to the streetlights
because we
are not
the ones
in flight
but returning
like dried-up
orange peels
to the dirt
again
and
again
empty-handed.

Demands

ELENA EISENSTADT

Nameless Courage

BECCA NORMAN

Hold my hand

As we walk down this aisle,

Lit by nothing but the flames of those who hate us.

They will shout,

They will spit,

They will swing,

We will walk, with our heads held high, silent in mourning.

The torches will burn, our eyes will sting.

Our grip will tighten as they try to pull us apart.

We will stay strong for those who could not.

We will walk, with our heads held high, loudly in triumph.

They will swing and spit and shout

While we, lit by nothing but the fire that sustains us,

Walk down this aisle, holding hands.

Dump and Burn

ISABELLA BROWN

To My Grandfather
My Introduction to Climate Organizing

LILY GARDNER

My grandfather never said "we should have," he always said "we will." So does my mother. These words do not come easily to me, a result of the inherent skepticism of my generation. We grew up in the midst of a climate crisis; it's hard to be optimistic about the future when the world is on fire.

In seventh grade, I learn the ice caps are melting, but the kids of the oil and gas executives complain. So just a week after learning the facts, we all sit down in neat little rows to absorb the lies:

UNPRECEDENTED GLOBAL WARMING IS NOT THE RESULT
OF HUMAN ACTIVITIES.

In the back of my mind, I know this refrain. I've seen it many times on the social media posts of friends, former teachers, and family members.

It's one year after my move from Salyersville, Kentucky, a tiny dot in the heart of Appalachia, to the suburbs of Lexington, an hour-and-a-half drive outside the mountains. I am from "coal country," but the coal industry has fled. Life in the mountains is all boom and bust and boom until one day, around the time I am born, everyone wakes up and can't hear the canary.

That summer, we drive to a different set of mountains, the Berkshires in Massachusetts, home to my maternal grandparents. I spend every summer there, in my family's house on the big hill.

The house is my grandmother's domain; my grandfather's: the garden. There, he teaches me the proper angle to snap the pea so it falls into my bucket below. He is a man who, despite his devotion to architecture of the built world, also cares deeply about the beauty of nature.

In the garden, blueberries fall into the pail. I take my commission early, sitting among the bushes, popping the fruit into my mouth. My grandfather is happy to continue picking. I am content watching his tender care for the natural world: a sense of duty that transcends his garden. This is one way he thinks to instill his values of conservation into all of us.

But I learn at an early age that my grandfather's environmentalism does not work in my Appalachian holler. This is a place where land equates to livelihood. The abstract choice to conserve land cannot compete with the practical need to put food on the table, regardless of the environmental consequences. I am keenly aware that the stakes in Salyersville are far greater than the quest for the perfectly ripe blueberry; the failures of the mainstream environmental movement in Appalachia were impossible to deny.

And then, in 2018, I find the Sunrise Movement.

Scrolling through Twitter, high on the wins of the midterm election, I am drawn to the shouts of young people crammed into Nancy Pelosi's office. I have never heard of a Green New Deal. But as I hear the words "Just Transition," I understand that their fight for climate justice is a movement that extends far beyond my grandfather's garden fence, perhaps even to my Appalachian home.

A week later, I am all in. Conversations with community leaders and rapid recruitment follow in quick succession. I feel a sense of possibility for my home and my state, my excitement a sharp contrast to the fatalism surrounding my Appalachian childhood.

When we hear that Senator Mitch McConnell is bringing the Green New Deal Resolution to a vote in February, we quickly hop on a plane and gather in the Capitol, ready to knock down his door. His vote to kill it is inevitable, but I am a conglomeration of cultures: an Appalachian Ashkenazi Jew. We know that action is not an option but a moral imperative. And so we drive.

Senator McConnell, I'm asking you to listen. Which side are you on?

Standing there, I am acutely aware that this is not the last time we will reckon with the deleterious effects of the climate change crisis. My generation grew up in a world on fire, yet we have the potential to build a world of dignity for all.

I stand on the shoulders of giants from my mountains, the union organizers who refused to back down. I come from resilient people who have fought for years to hold onto our cherished places.

My grandfather never said "we should have," he always said "we will." So does my mother. And as of late, so do I. At least, I'm learning to.

Upon the Dust of Our Ancestors

MICHAL SPANJER

We learn we are built upon the dust of our ancestors
Born with strength engraved into our DNA
We choose to evolve, growing from our mistakes
Carving our own footsteps into the path of history

We learn there is no harm in being afraid
Surrounded by oppression and hatred
We choose to be courageous
Standing proud in the midst of peril

We learn to embrace our tradition
Inheriting matzah and minor chords
We choose to be passionate
With everlasting, thunderous, irrational love

We learn to ask questions
Discuss the universe and all of its edges
We choose to wonder why we find ourselves here
Though we may never know the answer

We learn to be a community
United in our differences
We choose to transform our words into actions
And look toward a peaceful future

ARTIST STATEMENTS

***Eve*, Tesaneyah Dan** (p. 5): *Eve* is a charcoal portrait inspired by the third chapter of the book of Genesis in the Old Testament. It serves as an interpretation of the consequence passed down to the Mother of All the Living for being deceived by the serpent in the Garden of Eden, which has placed an undue burden on women, for they are made to carry the shame of Eve's wrongdoing. The apple in Eve's mouth works doubly to show her literal consumption of the fruit from the Tree of the Knowledge, and also to silence her. This consumption and her supposed persuasion of Adam to eat the fruit have caused her, and all women, to bear the guilt for the fall of man. The punishment of Eve continues to be evoked and has been used to dehumanize women, hence Eve having the eyes of the serpent.

***Held*, Alexa Druyanoff** (p. 6): My work explores where I come from, who came before me, and who I am. Portraits of lost relatives connect me to the past. Through the process of making art, I have gotten to know these relatives in my own way. I form these relationships through careful rendering: by shading their faces and following the curves of their cheekbones. The drawing process creates an intimacy that was stolen by war and the passage of time. I revive and retell family stories from my own perspective. I see my artistic role as both recorder and interpreter.

***Melting into Shards*, Liora Meyer** (p. 18): I took this photo in a beginner's photography class as an exercise in manipulating shutter speed. Originally, the photo reflected a moment of joy—the gleeful release of water and color in an indoor space. Each time I return to the photo, though, the droplets, frozen in time, mean something different to me.

***Barbara*, Leah Fleischer** (p. 22): The roses in front of my house were my inspiration for this piece. Barbara, a neighbor, always held whichever rose she picked tightly to her face and regarded the world with reddened eyes. She was a woman who could not freely love whom she wanted in my community. Love is hard enough on its own, but without the community's approval, it is even harder. Two people cannot build an entire world without support.

***No Worries*, Tali Feen** (p. 28): Always have big ideas. The little girl in this piece looks innocent holding a bunch of balloons as she crosses a bridge, but she's actually looking at the big city and creating her future. There is nothing that can stop her. Create your own dream and make it a reality.

***Serenity*, Aidyn Levin** (p. 36): I feel the most myself and the most peaceful in water. I'm able to stop time, push all my worries aside, and feel the smoothness of the water on my skin. I appreciate its cleansing power, both of my body and my soul. Water holds the power to connect me to myself and those in my life, and ultimately to a spiritual essence somewhere beyond.

***Labels*, Annie Poole** (p. 40): *Labels* reimagines high school stereotypes by digitally overlaying handwritten sticky notes on black-and-white portraits. Each subject portrays the emotion associated with their self-selected label and offers a possibility to escape it.

***Melting Head 34*, Eliana Shapere** (p. 56): This marker drawing is a colorful portrait of a melting head attached to a pair of blue legs. The background represents the chaos of movement in nature. I have been interested in the Surrealist movement for a while, and was inspired to try my hand at representing dreams and waking reality on the same page. The Surrealists believed in the power of accessing the unconscious mind through art, and I hope that this drawing will inspire its viewers to use their imaginations and create something beautiful. Although I drew this several years ago, I still have it hanging on my wall at home, and it's actually one of the pieces I'm most proud of.

Drowning, **Alex Berman** (p. 60): This piece reflects the weight of words. Like water, they may not seem to exert pressure, but they can easily drag you down.

Anxiety, **Aidyn Levin** (p. 64): Anxiety has always been a part of my life, and I wanted to represent it through a series of self-portraits. I used a piece of plastic wrap to try to illustrate the way I often feel trapped by my anxiety. For me, to be anxious is to feel like you're suffocating, to feel a knot in your stomach, to throw up; to be afraid of sneezing in class, of ordering at a restaurant, of making plans with friends. It is to go to therapy, to take medication, to practice deep breathing; to go months without the familiar gnawing feeling in your stomach, and then to suddenly feel like you're suffocating while you're studying for a math test. But it is also to learn to love yourself and all your quirks, to be proud of the progress you've made. Because although your anxiety is so much of who you are, you are not consumed by it.

Soft and Hard, **Alma Kastan** (p. 70): I created these two flower images when I was a junior in high school. I was taking a year-long photography class, and this was my final project. My intention was to combine something beautiful and delicate with sharp geometric shapes. Blending extreme opposites. Soft with harsh and, more obviously, black and white with color.

Me, Myself, and I, **Noa Kalfus** (p. 74): This is a series of self-portraits, each created using a different watercolor technique. Each portrait is unique but at the same time part of the greater "Noa," which reflects how I am a multifaceted and complex individual.

Free Woman, **Molly Voit** (p. 77): Vibrantly colorful, arms outstretched, hair caught in the wind, surrounded by the sun's warm glow, *Free Woman* tries to capture the feeling of being free of stress and worries.

The Art of Jewish Food, **Dalia Heller** (p. 84): For my confirmation project, I researched Jewish artists and completed a series of paintings of Jewish food that emulate the unique styles of those artists. I chose food as my subject because sharing food brings people together in celebration and across difference, and has been an integral part of Jewish holidays and events that are close to my heart. The pomegranates are done in the style of Marc Chagall, the bagels and lox in the style of Nachum Gutman. The latkes are in my own style, symbolizing my hope to carry on the tradition of Jewish artwork that has been passed down to me from world-renowned artists as well as artists in my own family, such as my great-grandfather and my Baubie, and countless others whose work lovingly portrays Jewish traditions, celebrations, history, family, and daily life.

Jazz, **Liora Meyer** (p. 92): This series works through the idea and practice of translation. I have used this project to explore the difficulty of capturing music in visual media. I chose to investigate the ways in which varying degrees of abstraction might more faithfully attempt that feat. Additionally, I used several media in order to get a fuller picture of how music might be expressed through the visual.

Eva, **Whitney Cohen** (p. 100): Eva Deutsch Costabel, a 96-year-old Holocaust survivor, renowned artist, published author/illustrator, and my personal friend, is depicted in charcoal and oil pastels. Eva is passionate about ensuring that her story and the stories of other survivors stay alive. She is originally from Zagreb,

Yugoslavia, where her father was ripped away by the Nazis to be deported and murdered in Treblinka. She then escaped with her mother and sister to Crikvenica, only to be imprisoned by the Italians in two camps (Kraljevica and Rab). In Rab, Eva worked as a nurse for the Yugoslav partisans (a Communist resistance group fighting the Axis powers in Yugoslavia) and spent much of her time secretly creating sketches of her surroundings. When her artistic talent was noticed by the partisans and she was placed in the propaganda unit, she fled to the Croatian coast, refusing to create Communist propaganda. Yad Vashem, the World Holocaust Remembrance Center, estimates that 66,000 out of 80,000 Yugoslav Jews died in the war. Eva often recognizes the irony in her artistic style of choice—bright and colorful abstract acrylic painting—which contrasts starkly with the tragedies that she has experienced. She has written and illustrated five published children's books, as well as a book of needlepoint designs. Eva became acquainted with my family in 2014 through my cousin's bar mitzvah project with the Blue Card, an organization that aids Holocaust survivors. She still attends our family b'nai mitzvah and yearly Pesach seders, and we are truly blessed to have her in our lives.

***Wit's End*, Annie Poole** (p. 110): I took a photo of an orange cone with the words "WITS END" that was in the middle of the street in New York City. Then I overlaid it with a photo of the new Hudson Yards development to contrast beginnings and endings.

***Feminine Strong*, Rachel Kaufman** (p. 117): I think a lot about the idea of being both feminine and strong. As someone with classically feminine traits, I have often been told that I seem ditsy and have felt that I have not been taken as seriously as people who seemed more masculine than I am. I think about how I can embrace my femininity and be a leader. For this piece, I used bright colors and bold brushstrokes to capture dried flowers and women whose femininity is imbued with confidence and strength.

***Kotel of My Dreams*, Dina Ocken** (p. 119): As an observant and egalitarian Jewish girl, I prefer to wear a tallit and to wrap tefillin when I pray every morning. But at the Kotel (the Western Wall in Jerusalem), which many consider the holiest site for Jews, women are highly discouraged from following such practices. Women of the Wall is a group of women who go to the Kotel every month and do exactly what I yearn to do: defy the notion that women cannot pray there however they choose. When I went to the Kotel last spring to participate in Women of the Wall, there was so much hatred between those women and the ultra-Orthodox community. In my painting, however, there is no barrier between the two groups. Both are free to pray at the Wall, in whichever way they prefer, because at the Kotel of my dreams, everyone is together, and people are united by their love of Judaism and prayer.

***Until Supreme Court Do Us Part*, Gertie Angel** (p. 124): I painted this piece because there are still numerous Supreme Court cases that challenge LGBTQ rights, including basic necessities such as health care and workplace protection. For many, it's scary to see basic human rights and personal futures hang in the balance of nine people's perspectives on what is "right."

***Mending the Broken*, Sonja Lippmann and Zoe Oppenheimer** (p. 131): Taken in New York City, San Francisco, and San Jose, this collection of photos depicts the movements for racial justice across the United States. The photo of the Martin Luther King Day march reflects the progress that has been made within the past century, while the photos of protests following the police killing of

148

George Floyd show how much work must still be done. Whether through peace or violence, the calls for a better future ring loud.

***Behind Bars,* Tali Feen** (p. 133): I used charcoal and soft pastel to create this piece.

***Say His Name, Say Their Names,* Gertie Angel** (p. 137): I made this digital art during the peak of the Black Lives Matter movement right after the murder of George Floyd. I wanted to show that although the movement was just gaining momentum, police brutality against Black and Brown people has always been a problem and has taken many lives.

***Demands,* Elena Eisenstadt** (p. 140): These are five photos I took at the first Women's March on Washington in 2017. I attempted to capture women's demands for the future when the present seemed perplexing and despondent. A woman wrote the words "Hands Off My" on a piece of poster board. Years later, women are still writing, saying, or screaming "Hands Off My," a demand that has been left unsatisfied.

***Dump and Burn,* Isabella Brown** (p. 142): I created this piece using colored pencils to showcase the aspects of climate change caused directly by human waste pollution, including harm to wildlife and the spread of toxic waste. This piece highlights how many major corporations have untenable solutions to the problem of waste management.

How to Use This Guide

The stories, poems, essays, and art in *Salt & Honey* give a glimpse into the lives of young women and nonbinary teens and how they grapple with identity, family, race, religion, and gender. The pieces are ripe for exploration with their powerful imagery and prose. This guide can be used to help you:

1. Read and reflect on your own.
2. Read and discuss with a friend.
3. Read in a group, such as a book club or class.

The guide has key questions to help you unpack each section. We have also shared activities to explore the pieces through your own art or writing, as well as "A Jewish Feminist Lens" that connects the pieces to the larger world of Jewish and feminist studies.

Chapter 1: We Always Seem to Return

Questions to Explore

1. In "Seeing Beyond," the writer shares the poignant story of her relationship with her sister. She says, "What I learned from Devora's brief but meaningful life is that it is important to put ourselves in other people's shoes. If we can only see the world through the lens of our own experiences, we will be stuck in a mindset that will never progress." Which perspectives in this chapter helped you see the world through a different lens?

2. A few pieces in this chapter explore the intersection of food and family. In "The Half-Mishpocha: Seeking Donor Sibs," the writer bonds with her new siblings over ice cream. In "Can You See God in a Grapefruit?" the writer connects with her mother by sharing a grapefruit. "Lemon Steam" is a whimsical story of a grandmother's recipe for lemon curd that suddenly transforms into butterflies and "takes off" in the narrator's imagination. Why do you think there is such a connection between food and family? Where do you see examples from your own life of fostering relationships at the dining room table?

3. Familial relationships are complicated. Some of the pieces in this chapter show positive bonds, such as "One," and others, like "Dad," show the pain that family can cause us. How do the writers embrace their families or rebel against them? What troubled you and what inspired you in this chapter? What was familiar to you, and what made you feel understood or less alone? What lessons can you draw from these narratives about how we live with our loved and not-so-loved ones?

A Jewish Feminist Lens

In "desired burden," the speaker focuses on the Kaddish prayer and the "superstitious women" who taught her mother to cook. Kaddish is the traditional mourner's prayer that praises God and asks God to create peace for all people. Traditionally, Kaddish is recited only by an immediate family member in order to keep away the "evil eye." Hence, the superstitious women who taught the speaker's mother to cook would not say the Kaddish. What are the superstitions in your own family? What have they taught you? For those of you who have experienced the loss of a family member, what rituals have brought you comfort?

Bring Your Creativity

In *Barbara*, the artist captures the beauty of aging. Create a painting, drawing, photograph, or collage inspired by your family that captures the beauty you see in aging and changing.

Doodle something here about a family member who has impacted your life.

Chapter 2: When We Were Small

Questions to Explore

1. In "Growing Up Girl" and "How to Label Yourself," the writers struggle with the expectations that come with being labeled a "girl" the moment they're born. By showing us their own struggles, they teach us how to rebel against the labels that others impose on us. What labels do you rebel against? What is the cost to you of being labeled? What expectations does society have for you that you are unwilling to embrace?

2. In "The Things I Should Have Said," the speaker gives us a glimpse of what regret feels like. She says, "these are the things I should have said / these are the things I wanted to say / these are the things I should have said, but didn't." Why do you think she didn't say these things? What stops you from saying what you feel? What do you wish you had said, but didn't?

3. In "tuesday night on a street corner, the speaker begins with, "I don't think she knows, / but she is the one who taught me what love is." Then the speaker paints a beautiful image of the first moments of falling in love, and concludes with, "rainbows dripped from her lips when she told me she loved me." How do you think the senses and falling in love are intertwined? When you reflect on your romantic experiences, what images come to mind?

Bring Your Creativity

In "You Bloom in the Art of Others," the writer follows the rich Jewish tradition of writing acrostics to grapple with the loss of her friend. Reflect on an experience from your own life that deeply shaped who you are, and write an acrostic to describe that experience.

Doodle something here that you have let go of as you have gotten older.

Chapter 3: A Healthy Collection of Hardships and Blessings

Questions to Explore

1. In "The Shape of Beauty: Reflections on an Adolescent Eating Disorder" and "A Letter to My Past Self," the writers share their heartbreaking struggles with eating disorders. What do these stories have in common? How are they different? What might you learn from them about how to find love for our bodies and strength within ourselves? What are some of the pressures specific to people in female-presenting bodies?

2. In "Pigtails Girl," the writer uses a surreal plot and style to capture the protagonist's emotional journey. Why do you think the writer chose this approach? How might surrealism describe life better than a straightforward telling? When you reflect on your own experiences involving powerful emotions, can you find anything surreal or "magical" about them?

3. The writers in this chapter share the struggles of being caught between childhood and adulthood as they grapple with relationships, gender identity, and responsibilities. For example, in "Fairy Poem," the narrator says, "When I wake up I am a weird brand of human: grown, scared, still tired, and eternally with a hint of dread. I seem to be rotting into one of those 'adults,' in the liminal space between fairyhood and adulthood—the purgatory between cotton-candy dreams and deadlines, lists, a harsh, concrete future." Which of these stories reflect your own experiences? Which challenge you to think differently about this moment in life?

A Jewish Feminist Lens

Ruth F. Brin (1921-2009) was a pioneer of Jewish feminist liturgy. She described her work as "a personal search for the ultimate reality, the wonder, the mystery, the meaning that most of us call God." The writers in this chapter follow in Brin's footsteps by reaching for meaning in their own lives and sometimes, boldly, naming what they find as divine. What ultimate reality do you search for? What does "God" mean to you?

Bring Your Creativity

In *Anxiety*, the artist uses several photos of herself to illustrate a single emotion. In *Me, Myself, and I*, the artist creates five self-portraits, each showing a different facet of herself. Using a similar approach, create a photo or image montage of yourself that captures a message you would like to share.

Write words of affirmation to yourself in the margins.

Chapter 4: Traditions, Interpretations, and Imperfections

Questions to Explore

1. Many of the pieces in this chapter describe the struggle of being Jewish in the modern world. Some of these writers have their Jewish identity questioned because of their skin color or their practice; others question their role in the community as their beliefs and practices evolve. What lessons did you learn from these pieces about resilience, community, power, and how we define Judaism for ourselves?

2. In "I Am Not Religious, Am I?" the writer describes her pathway to spirituality through music. She says, "Music has helped me soften the lines of my beliefs, proving that religion can be found through the beauty of sound, in science itself." When do you feel spiritual? How do your own passions enrich or complicate your Jewish identity?

3. Throughout Jewish history, there have been rituals from which women were excluded: wearing a tallit, wrapping tefillin, being counted as part of a minyan, studying certain Jewish texts. In "Because I Can," the speaker shares their inner dialogue as they wrap tefillin and claim this ritual for themselves. When have you felt excluded? How have you pushed back on limits to embrace the experiences that you care about?

A Jewish Feminist Lens

The first record of a boy becoming a bar mitzvah—a son of the commandments—was in the thirteenth century. However, it was not until 1922 that Judith Kaplan, the writer's great-great-aunt in "My Jewish-Themed Bat Mitzvah," became the first girl to celebrate becoming bat mitzvah: a daughter of the commandments. While the ceremony held a similar name to the boys' ceremony, Judith was not, in fact, allowed to read from the Torah scroll as boys were. That honor would take decades more to become a normal experience for girls in liberal Jewish communities, and even longer for girls in more traditional communities. Today Jewish communities are experimenting with new terms, such as *b-mitzvah* and *kabbalat mitzvah*, for ceremonies for teens who identify as nonbinary and are not comfortable being labeled as a girl or a boy. What have your experiences been with bar, bat, or b-mitzvah, either as a participant or a witness? What have you taken away from these experiences?

Bring Your Creativity

In "21st-Century Amidah," the speaker artfully combines the words of the traditional Amidah prayer with her own words. Choose a prayer or a poem that has meaning for you and imbue it with your own perspective.

Draw the symbols of your faith that are meaningful to you.

Chapter 5: Where Is the Peace?

Questions to Explore

1. In "Kyke Dyke," the speaker transforms a hateful, homophobic, anti-Semitic slur into a "battle cry," something she and her friends are proud to call themselves. How does this poem sit with you? How does it challenge your views of such language and the possibility of these offensive words to empower those most hurt by them?

2. Many of the stories in this chapter show the writers' frustration with the bigotry they are surrounded by. From the writer's rage at a racist shopkeeper in "Where Was the 'Peace' Four Hundred Years Ago?" to the writer's disdain for her anti-Semitic classmate in "What You See," this chapter shows us the devastating impact of injustice on our hearts and minds. Which pieces in this chapter did you find most disturbing? Which made you uncomfortable? Which will compel you to take action?

3. In "The Love You Carry," the writer says, "Suppressing my sexuality was like carrying a backpack of rocks. Each time I came out to a new person in my life, I took one rock out of the bag. Each time, I became lighter and a little bit closer to being airily, completely, incredibly free." Reflect on the pieces in this chapter. How do the authors free themselves of the weight of their worlds? How do you do this?

Bring Your Creativity

In "You Have Not Walked the Same Streets As Me," the speaker focuses on an experience she has had that she feels others have not shared. Reflect on an experience you have had that is unique to you or to a group that you are a part of. Write a poem about the metaphorical streets *you* have walked and the experiences *you* have known.

Doodle here words or images about issues that drive you to action.

Chapter 6: Carving Our Own Footsteps

Questions to Explore

1. In "To My Grandfather: My Introduction to Climate Organizing," the writer says, "My grandfather never said 'we should have,' he always said 'we will.' So does my mother. These words do not come easily to me, a result of the inherent skepticism of my generation." Where do you fall on this spectrum from optimism to skepticism for the future? What life experiences inform where you would place yourself?

2. This chapter centers on social justice issues of our time, from racial inequality to gun control to climate change. How do the perspectives presented in this chapter change the way you view these issues? Which of these issues are most important to you, and why?

3. In "Upon the Dust of Our Ancestors," the speaker says, "We learn we are built upon the dust of our ancestors / Born with strength engraved into our DNA." What strength is engraved in your DNA? Where does that strength come from? What does it drive you to do?

A Jewish Feminist Lens

The pursuit of justice has been at the center of Judaism since its biblical beginnings. In Deuteronomy 16:20 we are taught, "Justice, justice shall you pursue," and we are called to action by the prophet Amos (5:24), who taught, "Let justice roll down like a river, righteousness like a never-failing stream!" In the writings of the rabbis we are told, "On three things does the world stand: on justice, on truth, and on peace" (Pirkei Avot 1:18). Modern Jewish feminist leaders such as Ruth Bader Ginsburg, Gloria Steinem, and Emma Lazarus have embodied these principles by fighting for human rights, freedom, and self-determination for all people. Who are your role models for justice? What have they taught you?

Bring Your Creativity

In *Say His Name, Say Their Names*, the artist uses an ancient Jewish tradition of micrography—creating art with words—to capture the names of Black Americans killed through police violence. Examples of micrography include the words filling the picture (as the artist used here) or the lines of the image actually made of the words. Create a micrography using a text that you are passionate about.

Doodle in the margins what justice means to you.

RESOURCES

For more resources, please visit jgirlsmagazine.org/resources.

Alateen: Support for teens affected by someone else's alcoholism. al-anon.org/newcomers/teen-corner-alateen

AMAZE: Sex education for teens. amaze.org

Amudim: Support for individuals and families in the Jewish community impacted by sexual abuse, neglect, and addiction. amudim.org

Be'chol Lashon: Strengthens Jewish identity by raising awareness about the ethnic, racial, and cultural diversity of Jewish identity and experience. globaljews.org

Crisis Text Line: Mental health support and crisis intervention. crisistextline.org

Footsteps: Comprehensive services for people who have chosen to leave their ultra-Orthodox Jewish communities. footstepsorg.org

HereNow: A teen-led community and app for mental health.

Jews in All Hues: Support for Jews of color and multiple-heritage Jews. jewsinallhues.org

JQY: Support for LGBTQ Jewish youth. jqyouth.org

Keshet: Advances LGBTQ equality in Jewish life through educator training, queer youth empowerment, and civil rights advocacy. keshetonline.org

Matan: Enables Jewish professionals and families to create inclusive Jewish educational, communal, and spiritual settings. matankids.org

NEDA: Support for individuals and families affected by eating disorders. nationaleatingdisorders.org

National Institute on Drug Abuse for Teens: Information about the effects of drug use on teens. teens.drugabuse.gov

National Suicide Prevention Lifeline: 24/7 support for people in suicidal crisis or emotional distress. suicidepreventionlifeline.org, 1-800-273-8255

No Shame on U: Breaks the stigma associated with mental health conditions in the Jewish community and beyond. noshameonu.org

OK2Talk: Support for young adults struggling with mental health conditions. ok2talk.org

RAINN: Anti-sexual violence organization. rainn.org

SOJOURN: Support for the Jewish LGBTQ+ community across the South. sojourngsd.org

Stop Sexual Assault in Schools: Education for students, families, and schools about the right to education free from sexual harassment. stopsexualassaultinschools.org

Teen Line: Teen-to-teen education and support before problems become a crisis. teenlineonline.org

Teens Against Bullying: Support for middle school and high school students against bullying. pacerteensagainstbullying.org

18Doors: Support for people in interfaith relationships—individuals, couples, families and their children—who want to engage in Jewish life. 18doors.org

ACKNOWLEDGMENTS

I am a well of gratitude for all those who have made this book and jGirls Magazine possible.

Everyone who has been involved with jGirls has had a role in making it a success. To our teen staff and alums throughout the years: no one could have prepared me for the magnitude of your extraordinariness. I am humbled and proud to work with you. Thank you for sharing my vision, making it your own, and being my partners in building our space.

A number of teen staff members and alums need special mention given their work to make this book a reality. Annie Poole, Emanuelle Sippy, and Maya Savin Miller, your feedback and ideas were instrumental in crafting the book's proposal. Emanuelle and Maya, thank you for your genius in conceiving of the book's arc and structure, and for being my writing partners on the chapter introductions. Your talents have immeasurably expanded the capacity of this book to serve as a source of reflection and connectedness. Audrey Honig and Aydia Caplan, I am grateful to you for adding specificity, care, joy, and thoughtfulness to those introductions. Cecelia Ross, Elena Eisenstadt, Lily Pazner, and Reggie Hopkins, as well as Aydia, Emanuelle, and Maya, thank you for your insight and tirelessness in combing through all the creative, important work we have received over the years to select the pieces for this volume. Aidyn Levin, Alex Berman, Dalia Heller, Joelle Reiter, Naomi Kitchen, Sonja Lippmann, and Zoe Lanter, thank you for your fresh, nuanced feedback and ideas. And thank you to all our 2019-2020 and 2020-2021 teen editors and photographers who gave energy, time, and creativity to this process.

To all our teen contributors and community members, including those not represented in these pages, thank you for entrusting jGirls with your fullest voices and most authentic selves.

I am so fortunate to work with talented, creative, compassionate, and delightful adult staff members and consultants. Michele Lent Hirsch, thank you for working with me on the book proposal, and also for being a partner in writing the chapter introductions. It has been so much fun thinking and writing with you, and I have learned tremendously. Carolyn Kettig, our program director, thank you for making everything "bestiful" and expanding exponentially what jGirls can be. Annie Poole and Sara Bogomolny, thank you for bringing your sense of design and style to this work. Shani Leead and Meredith Wolf Schizer, thank you for keeping us up and running. Audrey Honig, thank you for vision in shaping our alum work. Izzy Wellman, it's been a pleasure to welcome you. Dr. Sharon Weiss-Greenberg and Jennifer Lewin, thank you for making this organization, and me, stronger.

I am enriched personally and professionally by jGirls' advisors—formal and informal—and other close friends. Katina Paron, I am grateful to you for answering an email from a near stranger, helping me to move from an idea to a reality, and shaping our foundation—and, together with Michele, helping to craft the book proposal. Dr. Andrea Jacobs and Julie Sissman, friends, coaches, mentors: thank you for always answering the phone and for seeing the full me. Aliza Mazor and Esther Kustanowitz, you challenge me to be better and think bigger. Rabbi Kara Tav and Ella Tav, you are visionaries, dreamers, role models for mother-daughter relationships. Boris Kievsky, thank you for your guidance from the earliest days. Ariele Mortkowitz and Sara Shapiro-Plevan, this journey has gotten infinitely better since our roads merged. Dr. Jordana Jaffee, thank you for attaching yourself to this project, and for being my BFF for so very many years. I wouldn't be me without you. Dr. Shana Sippy, thank you for bringing your expertise to this work.

Tani Prell, Tova Harris, Dr. Betsy Stone, and Dr. Andrea Jacobs, thank you for your wisdom and guidance in making this book more thoughtful and inclusive.

Molly Tolsky and Michelle Shapiro Abraham, I am so grateful to you for framing this book so beautifully. Allie Alperovich, my friend and counsel, and the team at Ropes & Gray, thank you for your sage advice and steady hand.

To publisher David Behrman and executive editor Dena Neusner at Behrman House, I am forever grateful to you for believing in this project, for recognizing and honoring the voices contained in these pages, and for the opportunity to work together. To my talented, thoughtful, patient editor, Alef Davis, it's been a true privilege to go through this process with you. Zahava Bogner, thank you for your thoughtfulness and creativity, Vicki Weber, thank you for raising the profile of this book. And Aviva Gutnick, thank you for bringing jGirls Magazine to the attention of Behrman House after a semi-chance encounter on an airport jitney. This book would not exist without all of you.

Thank you to all of our donors, including founding donor Sally Gottesman, the Covenant Foundation, FJC, the Good People Fund, the Hadassah Foundation, the Jewish Education Project/UJA-Federation of NY, Women of Vision—Jewish Federation of Greater Philadelphia, the Jewish Women's Foundation of Metropolitan Chicago, the Jewish Women's Foundation of New York, the Jewish Women's Fund of Atlanta, The Morty Frank Memorial Fund, Slingshot, UpStart, and all of our individual supporters. We could not do this work without you. Thank you for your belief in me and in jGirls, and for all the work you do to make our community stronger and more equitable.

Thank you, thank you, to my family: to my husband, Steven, for always believing in me, encouraging my ideas, supporting me in innumerable ways, and showing me unconditional love. To my parents, Dr. Harvey and Harriet Mandel, for making sure I knew that girls could be anything they wanted to be. To my sisters, Dr. Aly Mandel, a brilliant child psychologist who makes everything clearer, and who provides important perspective and counsel on our work at jGirls and on this book particularly; and Ariane Mandel, for always holding my hand, making me laugh, and bringing food and cats.

And last but not least, to my three powerful, funny, wise, delicious children, Gertie, Penelope, and Matilda. When people ask me why I started jGirls, I start off by answering, "Well, I have three daughters…." You inspire me every minute of every day to do what I can to make the world a better place for you, for all of our daughters, for all of our children. Thank you for standing up for yourselves, for speaking out for others, and for changing my life. I love you madly and forever.

Elizabeth Mandel
founder and executive director, jGirls Magazine

ABOUT JGIRLS MAGAZINE

jGirls Magazine is a pluralistic, online global community for self-identifying female and nonbinary Jewish teenagers to voice their realities, engage with new ideas, lift each other up, and lead social change.

Our content is created by Jewish teens ages thirteen to nineteen, curated and edited by a teen editorial board, and shaped by teen staff photographers. Our community is diverse in background, perspective, Jewish identification, sexual orientation, gender identity and expression, race, ethnicity, and ability. The work we publish exemplifies the rich, varied, and vivid experiences of Jewish teenagers from around the world.

We welcome submissions of articles, essays, opinion pieces, short stories, poetry, cultural reviews, humor, photography, videos, music, artwork, and other creative materials at any time of year. Contributors whose work is accepted receive peer edits and are compensated for their work upon publication.

Each year we invite teens entering tenth, eleventh, and twelfth grades from throughout North America to apply to join the jGirls feminist leadership development program and to serve as staff editors and photographers. Teen staff members engage with a community of peers to hone communication skills, share challenges and victories, explore identities, talk across differences, and prepare to become the future of Jewish leadership. Teen staff members receive a stipend for their participation.

Want to know more? Please visit jgirlsmagazine.org or reach out to us at info@jgirlsmagazine.org. We look forward to hearing from you!

Elizabeth Mandel is the founder and executive director of jGirls Magazine. She is an award-winning documentary filmmaker, writer, editor, and community activist. Elizabeth has built a record of using media to raise awareness and create change around social justice, gender, and Jewish community issues. Her films have screened on public television and at organizations and film festivals around the world. Mandel holds a BA in religion and a master's in international affairs, with a focus on women's economic and political development, both from Columbia University. She lives in New York with her husband and three daughters.

Emanuelle Sippy codirected the Kentucky Student Voice Team and led the jGirls Magazine art department throughout high school. She continues to treasure and support these communities while studying at Princeton University and organizing with Future Coalition. Originally from California, Emanuelle grew up in Minneapolis and now calls Lexington, Kentucky home.

Maya Savin Miller is dedicated to the regeneration of our social and ecological soils through poetry, education, and farming. She was the head of the jGirls poetry department while in high school, and her writing has been recognized by dozens of literary journals and competitions. Born and raised in Los Angeles, Maya would always prefer to be in the mountains.

Michele Lent Hirsch is a writer, editor, and creative writing teacher whose work has appeared in the *Atlantic*, the *Guardian*, and the *Bellevue Literary Review*, among other outlets. Her first book, *Invisible*, a blend of journalism and memoir on gender, health, and inequity, came out in 2018 from Beacon Press.

Molly Tolsky is the founder and editor of Hey Alma, a Jewish feminist website from 70 Faces Media. She holds a BA in fiction writing from Columbia College Chicago and an MFA in fiction writing from Sarah Lawrence College. Her writing can be found in *Tin House, Hayden's Ferry Review*, Electric Literature, and elsewhere. She is also senior editor of No Tokens.

Michelle Shapiro Abraham, RJE, has worked in the field of Jewish education for over twenty years and currently serves as the director of learning and innovation for the Union for Reform Judaism's youth team. She is a PJ Library and Sydney Taylor Notable Book Award author and the proud recipient of the 2015 Covenant Award for Excellence in Jewish Education.

***

Aliza Abusch-Magder is from California. She enjoys reading in the sun and angsty teen pop, and she is a confident yet terrible dancer.

Lauren Alexander is from Florida. She loves singing and advocating for social justice issues, specifically those surrounding the disabled community.

Gertie Angel is from New York. She loves painting, reading, writing, and cooking.

Yael Beer is from New York. They love knitting and making up fun stories with their friends, and they have a knack for picking up languages.

Alex Berman is from New York. Alex likes running and playing DnD, and has a debilitating obsession with old ships.

Alyx Bernstein is from New York. She likes watching soccer, studying Talmud, and playing Jewish geography with celebrities.

Leah Bogatie is from Ontario. She enjoys reading novels and playing her guitar, and she tends to notice the details in the world around her.

Isabella Brown is from Michigan. She loves drawing and reading, and she has dedicated a substantial portion of her life to memorizing facts about sharks.

Aydia Caplan is from Colorado. She loves weaving stories through both writing and acting, and she is a Bananagrams virtuoso.

Whitney Cohen is from New York. She enjoys mixed media art, playing with her cat, Phoebe Buffay, and telling people about her leap day birthday.

Emilia Cooper is from New York. She enjoys working with children, and she has been traveling abroad by herself since she was fifteen years old.

Tesaneyah Dan is from New York. She enjoys writing stories and drawing. The focus of her work is the intersection of Black womanhood and Torah.

Denae is from New York. They love to dance and sing, and they have a knack for learning how to code.

Alexa Druyanoff is from California. She loves illustrating for her school newspaper, painting her family, and skiing in Deer Valley.

Emily Duckworth is from North Carolina. She loves reading and running, and she's known to make a mean rhubarb pie.

Elena Eisenstadt is from Pennsylvania. She has a strange love for unreliable public transportation and refuses to wear jewelry that isn't her mom's.

Tali Feen is from Georgia. She loves to go on runs to free her mind and cannot wait to be a pediatric cardiovascular surgeon.

Abigail Fisher is from New York. She enjoys writing plays, short stories, and personal essays, and she has a particular affection for inky pens.

Leah Fleischer is from Maryland. She enjoys dressing as a ghost. She's good at making up whimsical images for stories and designs for clothing.

Lily Gardner is from Kentucky. She loves listening to movie soundtracks and frequently needs to pee.

Abigael Good is from New Jersey. She loves fantasy books and silly TV shows, and she studies queer Jewish things.

Sequoia Hack is from California. She enjoys baking and city walks. She has an unusual loyalty to iced drinks and an unusual opposition to hot drinks.

Madison Hahamy is from Illinois. She loves rewatching television shows and writing for various publications, and she has a twin brother.

Samara Haynes is from New Jersey. She enjoys rowing on her school's crew team and serves as her district's representative to the board of education.

Ahava Helfenbaum is from Toronto. She enjoys yoga and hanging out with her dog Cody, and she loves all things coffee.

Dalia Heller is from Illinois. She plays the flute, enjoys painting and drawing, and loves to learn history and foreign languages.

Sasha Hochman is from Pennsylvania. She enjoys studying history. Parks, picnics, and puzzles consume much of her free time.

Audrey Honig is from Illinois. She loves Jewish summer camp and playing her purple accordion.

Alexa Hulse is from North Carolina. She loves Mary Oliver and crafting, and she is particularly good at remembering birthdays.

Liel Huppert is from Minnesota. She enjoys fantasy novels and snuggling with her cats. She is a huge fan of anime.

Noa Kalfus is from New York. She loves science and art, and she has a nearly encyclopedic knowledge of 2000s comedy shows.

Alma Kastan is from New York. She loves exploring the city, listening to music, and going shopping with friends. She always enjoys making pottery.

Rachel Kaufman is from Idaho. She loves skateboarding, drinking tea, painting, and, most importantly, hanging out with her cats.

Maya Keren is from Pennsylvania. She loves Erykah Badu a lot. She aspires to be able to dunk a basketball one day.

Naomi Kitchen is from Pennsylvania. She loves to travel and watch movies, and she moved to Israel upon her high school graduation.

Gavi Klein is from California. She loves playing guitar and reading, and she once spent three months working on a goat farm.

Jamie Klinger is from New Jersey. She enjoys history, museums, and extensively reviewing television for friends.

Emily Knopf is from New Jersey. She loves playing the ukulele, especially to her bunnies, and she is an unusually good Hula-Hooper.

Aidyn Levin is from Georgia. She loves checking books off of her endless reading list and has watched *Grey's Anatomy* more times than anyone should.

Sonja Lippmann is from California. She loves exploring new places with friends and family, and she has become unusually skilled at recalling her dreams.

Shoshana Maniscalco is from Massachusetts. She enjoys trying new craft projects and can often be found teaching Hebrew and rock climbing.

Liora Meyer is from Massachusetts. She loves strength training and exploring cities, and she is unusually good at ordering from new restaurants.

Becca Norman is from Connecticut. They love to read and garden, and they have an intense love for science, specifically ecology.

Juliet Norman is from Florida. She is obsessed with astrology and never misses an episode of *Saturday Night Live*.

Dina Ocken is from New York City. She loves playing Ultimate Frisbee, studying math and science, and talking about egalitarian Judaism.

Zoe Oppenheimer is from New York. She loves exploring new places, and so far, she has been to thirty-seven countries.

Lily Pazner is from Michigan. She loves to dance around her kitchen while she bakes, and her favorite word is *petrichor*, since she loves thunderstorms.

Annie Poole is from Washington. She enjoys living in New York City and exploring art museums and thrift shops, and she is impressively clumsy.

Ofek Preis is from New York. She loves experimenting with music, fashion, and makeup, and she has even dyed her own hair twelve times in one year.

Maya Rabinowitz is from Pennsylvania. She loves baking pies and spending time with her dog, Charlie.

Emma Rosman is from Virginia. She loves trying new foods, working out, and hanging out with her four dogs.

Cecelia Ross lives in Ohio. She enjoys playing the cello and drawing, and she is fascinated by brains.

Sydney Schulman is from New York. She writes about anything from astrology to college parties, and she is working to hike the forty-six Adirondack High Peaks.

Eliana Shapere is from Kentucky. She loves music and writing. She knows just enough Russian to order food in Brighton Beach.

Michal Spanjer is from Indiana. She loves taking pictures and cooking with friends, and she has been writing songs since she was six years old.

Frankie Vega is originally from Colorado and now resides in California. She loves to design clothing and stare down little dogs at dog parks.

Molly Voit is from New York. She enjoys making art and traveling with her friends, and she is skilled on a scooter.

Abigail Winograd is from Georgia. She loves cooking and runs a plant-based meal delivery service and recipe blog.

Sarah Young is from upstate New York. She enjoys reading, writing, and cross-stitching bad puns.

Makeda Zabot-Hall is from Maine. She enjoys writing and being around her friends and family. She has a passion for social justice.